Twin Peaks: The Return, Part 8

TIMECODES

A book series exploring individual movies minute by minute.

Series Editors

Nicholas Rombes, University of Detroit Mercy, USA
Nadine Boljkovac, University of Colorado, USA

Advisory Board

Paweł Frelik (University of Warsaw, Poland)
Andrew Gallix (Independent Scholar, France)
Colleen Kennedy-Karpat (Bilkent University, Turkey)
Shiva Moghanloo (Independent Scholar, Iran)
Björn Sonnenberg-Schrank (Heinrich Heine University
Düsseldorf, Germany)
Steven Shaviro (Wayne State University, USA)
Constantine Verevis (Monash University, Australia)

Also in the Series:

BlacKkKlansman: Movies Minute by Minute, by
Alex Zamalin
Gerry: Movies Minute by Minute, by Nicholas Rombes

Twin Peaks: The Return, Part 8

Movies Minute by Minute

Jeff Wood

BLOOMSBURY ACADEMIC

NEW YORK · LONDON · OXFORD · NEW DELHI · SYDNEY

BLOOMSBURY ACADEMIC
Bloomsbury Publishing Inc, 1359 Broadway, New York, NY 10018, USA
Bloomsbury Publishing Plc, 50 Bedford Square, London, WC1B 3DP, UK
Bloomsbury Publishing Ireland, 29 Earlsfort Terrace, Dublin 2, D02 AY28, Ireland

BLOOMSBURY, BLOOMSBURY ACADEMIC and the Diana logo are trademarks of
Bloomsbury Publishing Plc

First published in the United States of America 2025

Copyright © Jeff Wood, 2025

Epigraph on p.v © Sam Shepard, 1981

Cover design: Eleanor Rose
Cover illustration © Freya Betts

All rights reserved. No part of this publication may be: i) reproduced or transmitted in
any form, electronic or mechanical, including photocopying, recording or by means of
any information storage or retrieval system without prior permission in writing from
the publishers; or ii) used or reproduced in any way for the training, development or
operation of artificial intelligence (AI) technologies, including generative AI technologies.
The rights holders expressly reserve this publication from the text and data mining
exception as per Article 4(3) of the Digital Single Market Directive (EU) 2019/790.

Bloomsbury Publishing Inc does not have any control over, or responsibility for, any
third-party websites referred to or in this book. All internet addresses given in this
book were correct at the time of going to press. The author and publisher regret any
inconvenience caused if addresses have changed or sites have ceased to exist, but
can accept no responsibility for any such changes.

Library of Congress Cataloging-in-Publication Data
Names: Wood, Jeff (Novelist) author
Title: Twin Peaks : the return, part 8: movies minute by minute / Jeff Wood.
Description: New York : Bloomsbury Academic, 2025. | Series: Timecodes | Includes
bibliographical references and index.
Identifiers: LCCN 2025015175 | ISBN 9798765121740 hardback | ISBN
9798765121757 paperback | ISBN 9798765121771 pdf | ISBN 9798765121788 epub
Subjects: LCSH: Twin Peaks (Television program : 2017) | LCGFT: Television
criticism and reviews
Classification: LCC PN1992.77.T88 W66 2025 | DDC 791.45/72--dc23/eng/20250411
LC record available at https://lccn.loc.gov/2025015175

ISBN: HB: 979-8-7651-2174-0
PB: 979-8-7651-2175-7
ePDF: 979-8-7651-2177-1
eBook: 979-8-7651-2178-8

Series: Timecodes

Typeset by Deanta Global Publishing Services, Chennai, India

For product safety related questions contact productsafety@bloomsbury.com.

To find out more about our authors and books visit www.bloomsbury.com and sign up
for our newsletters.

*There's gonna be a general lack of toast in the
neighborhood this morning.*
—SAM SHEPARD, TRUE WEST

CONTENTS

Introduction 1

Minutes 1–56 13

Postscript 105

Notes 106
Index 121

Introduction

The Way the Crow Flies

26 miles southwest of Columbus, Ohio on Interstate 71 stands a lone and aging billboard calling out to all travelers. In white letters painted on a black field—with one scarlet "H"—the billboard reads: HELL IS REAL.

When I was a child, we would pass the billboard on our way to visit my great-grandmother in Middletown, Ohio. I'd gaze warily out the car window and watch the ominous words floating by: HELL IS REAL. That was all it said. But so much was contained in the transmission of those three oversized words. *What did it mean?* And how did that meaning vibrate on a shockwave of such silent tremor that it sent the entire landscape listing? Were these *words* at all? Or was this phrase some kind of cinematic demonstration of itself—something *animate*? Of some kind of *agency*? Was I reading or *watching*? Should I have looked away? If the words entered my eyes—as they inevitably did—would it make them true? Either way, it was too late. *The sign caught me looking, and I saw it looking back.* And I was implicated in that loop, initiated into a kind of terrifying voodoo of language: a black magic of words; of a code that generates its own circuit of reality, suspended somewhere in the nebulous confluence of the fictional and the real—the poem, the hymn, the *Hallmark* card, and the lie, the malevolent AI—a stark message delivered in the *genre* of some dark advertising, screaming silently across the yellowing soybeans, itself recursive proof of its claim. HELL IS REAL. That rogue and spectral road sign is, in my estimation, among the most important works of land art in the country, an aphoristic prophecy in the *cinematic* vernacular of America from one century to the next.

Head due south of the infernal billboard, and drawn above the river in the trees is another kind of primal sign that even its makers could not see: the Great Serpent Mound of Ohio, a 2,000-year-old earthwork depicting a snake devouring an egg. This twilight prehistoric landform is among the most extraordinary on earth—for the artistry of its spiraling tail and undulating wavelengths traveling the length of four football fields; for the mythic ambiguity of its *purpose;* and perhaps most significantly, for the curious fact that none of its engineers could have ever possibly *seen* it, from above, or at all, but in a dream, in the television of their own collective mind's eye: an endurance-length, geoglyphic cinema of sorts, progressing in still-life stop-action, frame by frame across the screen of time itself. For whom? Themselves, from an astral point of view: a Google Earth, offline. Or perhaps for aliens out here in *this* future: time-travelers who would one day observe their embossed, serpentine representation in this now.

Bear northeast of the Great Snake the way the crow flies, and you may come upon what remains of its forsaken garden—an abandoned office building east of Columbus: the Longaberger Basket Building, a now-shuttered corporate headquarters constructed in the precise likeness of a gigantic picnic basket. Unlike the Great Serpent Mound, this feat of aesthetic engineering is quite visible to its contemporaries flying in and out of east central Ohio. From an aerial point of view, the impossibly oversized folk object triggers a total disorientation of scale and is rendered impossibly *miniature* upon the GMO'd pastoral landscape; a cultural artifact so grotesquely over-scaled that it appears tiny. Back on the ground, the giant picnic basket is now devoured by uselessness—a literal roadside picnic as an exclusionary zone—but for its absurd symbolic time signature as a building-sized Jeff Koons,[1] or the Zone of an American cultural economy emanating the glitching representation of itself—the iconographic loop of an apocalyptic kitsch: that symbol that has reached its dead end *and can only mean itself*.

North by northwest returning, my own hometown of Delaware, Ohio lies along the banks of the Olentangy River, a tributary of the Scioto and Ohio River Valleys, and, as the names imply, a once-dynamic Native American watershed preceding the opening of the American West.[2] Delaware's historic movie house—The Strand Theatre—opened in 1916 and is one of the ten longest-operating movie theaters in the country. It was there at The Strand in 1977, at the age of seven, that I first saw *Star Wars*,[3] a popcorn movie improbably spanning the entire history of cinema—in theme, story, genre, score, production design, acting style, and above all, marketing—and consequently, a harbinger[4] of things to come, casting its silver shadow to the ends of the earth and devouring the world as its own memetic future: its *future fiction*, or the fiction of the world as ubiquitously distributed *medium* and genre-annihilating *content* alike, the cinematic prototype of a magically streaming science-fiction future-apparatus, a fictional real within which we now fully reside.

Premiering two months earlier in that same year, to significantly less fanfare (twenty-five people in a single theatre in Los Angeles), was David Lynch's first feature film, *Eraserhead*, its own kind of auteur and fantastical family melodrama. *Star Wars* and *Eraserhead*—a double feature for the ages. One, an intergalactic *space opera*; the other a subterranean, cosmic interiority. Each in possession of astonishing artistry and design, as total inversions of each other, yet exemplary of a binary precipice to the 1980s, overlooking a vast uncanny valley of cultural *production values* and a vigorous cognitive dissonance in the kinds of stories it would come to tell itself about who and what it is. By the middle of the decade, Lynch would elevate that collective cognitive dissonance from the level of subtext to a dramatic and disturbing visual text, disrupting the American cinematic vernacular with his *Blue Velvet* (1986). He would then ring in a new decade by transforming the psychology of television itself—an entire in-home medium—with *Twin Peaks*.

Anchoring itself to the foundational television mythology (and cliché) of an American small town setting, 1990s *Twin Peaks* tapped into a fascination with the stereotypes of rural isolation and idiosyncrasy, recapitulated as a lingering 1980s frontier Americana; the accompanying fetish of a backwoods mysticism; its transgressions and trafficking in illicit economy, addiction, and sexual violence; the vestigial remnants of its vast prehistoric context—*its nature*; and a counter-intervention by the Feds—or an archetypal FBI—with its own twin ethos of just and transparent reason and a *classified* deep state bureaucracy-unto-paranormality. These signatory themes of a *Twin Peaks* dramaturgy would eventually swell through an entire media ecosystem, exploiting and capitalizing on those internal propensities toward demographic, cultural, and political otherness, a tsunami of contemporary media that by 2017—and the *Return* of *Twin Peaks*—would amalgamate into a monstrous compound information entity all its own, one that would ultimately challenge any remaining firewalls between fiction, reality, and their co-conspiratorial engineering as *total fiction* or a conspiracy of the real.

^o^

The geographic center of the contiguous United States is located at 39°50'N, 98°35'W, near the town of Lebanon, Kansas. According to Walter Murch, the legendary editor of *Apocalypse Now!*, director Francis Ford Coppola had wanted his 1979 operatic and psychedelic Vietnam War epic to screen permanently at a dedicated movie theatre established at that geographic center of the country. There, *Apocalypse Now!* would be installed as a geographic monument and pilgrimage site to America's legacy of violent delirium—its own heart of darkness—a *cinematic monument* to the phantasmagoric crucible of a violently cinematic country whose shared means of knowing itself, and its violence as *content,* is the screen. Kansas too, of course, is the fabled setting of *The Wizard of Oz*, the 1939 national treasure well-documented as being among David Lynch's core references, a nesting of narrative structures that would serve Lynch's own fevered imagination. Here, at the symbolic center of the country again, an animatronic illusion or fraudulence is revealed behind theatrical curtains, inside a fantastic musical dream, inside the overwhelming power and trauma of nature—or *acts of God*[5]—all from the perspective of a young girl. *The Wizard of Oz* is a kind of American ur-film, exemplifying a *cinematic position* of cultural idealism, or magic: the total liturgical voodoo invested in the narrative *meme* of our ruby slippers, the bedazzled and totemic fetish objects of the cultural economy without which there is apparent chaos, labor, fortune or misfortune, and forces both cosmic and bureaucratic beyond our comprehension or control. *Twin Peaks: The Return* (and Part 8 in particular, as we will see) is Lynch's own kind of sequel to that cinematic voodoo at the far ends of the yellow brick road, now a broken painted line on the highway, a repeating signal of broken Morse code.

Just a few hours east of Lebanon (and that mythic geo-coordinate) is Lawrence, Kansas, eventual home to William S. Burroughs, Lynch's senior fellow traveler in the avant-garde of a surreal, paranormal, and nightmarish American id. Burroughs, and his prolific Pacific Coast contemporary, Philip K. Dick, navigated paranoid and altered states—whether induced by the self or by the State—as symptoms of necessary dissociation from the power, psychosis, and techno-magic of its human appendage, the American cultural economy as a self-surveilling apparatus.[6] The problem with being paranoid is that all things are in fact connected. For Lawrence, Kansas was also the setting for the TV movie *The Day After*.

Premiering on national network television on November 20, 1983, the day after my thirteenth birthday, *The Day After* is among the most-watched events in television history. Dramatizing the catastrophic sequence and immediate after-effects of a nuclear exchange between the United States and the Soviet Union, *The Day After* stunned an audience of over 100 million viewers with its unflinching dramatic realism and the searing otherworldly *surrealism of that apocalyptic realism*. The shocking x-ray effect of human skeletons flaring through a translucent membrane of living bodies is burned into my own memory as civilian bystanders one and all—children, grandparents, pets, livestock—were caught in the sudden flash of nuclear strike. In that melting of an on-screen dramatic realism into molten horror, it was media itself that was becoming liquid, and eventually liquid crystal, melting into a living mirror at the reactor core of perception. Was *The Day After* a speculative science fiction or the documentary of a certain future? Was this Reality TV—a theatrical fiction contrived, yet somehow also real? Was it *news?* An event *lived-with*, yet invisible and perpetual: *a simultaneity* into which at any moment reality might combust. Or was it the propaganda of a culture herding itself into engineered, collective identification? *The Day After* was all of the these things—as states of being, as modes of perception, as *genre*—initiating a permanent inflection and conflation of media and the real into a traumatic *cinematic real*.

The result of that television event was not the engendering of a naive belief in fictions but a counter-suspicion in the integrity of lived reality itself, as an exchange between the two states—*in which they are each other*—an osmotic transference between a so-called theatrical fourth wall (as suspension of disbelief) into a nascent neurological *fifth wall* of the totally fictional real, a replicant real, and the eventual physiological apparatus of a collective nervous system vulnerable to it. The really occurring apocalypse of November 1983 was an *apocalypse of apocalypse*, a lifting of the veil onto a future media-apparatus capable of recapitulating and infusing apocalypse into the very fabric of the culture *as* the fabric of that culture—apocalypse as a *feature* of the culture itself, as a mode of seeing and being: apocalypse as de facto cultural disposition. In its potency at liquifying categories of representation, *The Day After* even came with a horrifying end-credits disclaimer, not disclaiming and asserting itself as fiction, but decrying the fact that it was incapable of being real enough: *"The catastrophic events you have just witnessed are, in all likelihood, less severe than the destruction that would actually occur in the event of a full nuclear strike against the United States,"* it read. It goes without saying—but must be said—that the severity of that destruction and suffering would extend well beyond the United States, as a total event, marked by total and totally systemic terror.

Theorist Paul Virilio describes this specific mode of total ambient terror as *cosmic fear*—a fear that has no locational origin or source, but is initiated by a collapse of geographic space. Cosmic fear is immediate, imminent, and interior; everywhere and nowhere; inside experience itself, suffusing a perception of experience as each and every atomic pixel of the world into an omnipresent *saturation* of fear initiated by "the nuclearization of the world."[7] "The first real and symbolic explosion in Hiroshima," he observes, "opened the space of cosmic fear."[8] Real: as the historic event itself initiated the existential threat of real annihilation; and symbolic: as the detonation of the world into an instantaneous globalized contraction, in which there is nowhere to go, nowhere to escape, nowhere to hide. There is no elsewhere now. "Fear, as a product of spatio-temporal contraction, has paradoxically become cosmic. . . . Cosmic in the sense of space-time: fear now covers the relationship to the universal."[9] We are acutely familiar by now with the cosmic contraction of individual experience as a kind of remote intimacy—a personalized, globalized anxiety, mediated and maintained, of course, by the internet. For we have reached, Virilio concludes, *"not the end of history but the end of geography."*[10] There is also here. "The world is foreclosed,"[11] and already (how quickly! how instantly!) "we are now at the end of the digital. I cannot accept being enclosed in numbers, numerological cult."[12] A world without distance, intolerably *enclosed* as QR-code, is a claustrophobia of no outside at all. A Rorschach-type pattern that promises to deliver recognition and passage, but only leads to more code. It is into the numerological cult of that ghost geo-coordinate, buried deeper and deeper within a collapsing interiority, that Lynch's *Twin Peaks: The Return* will magnetically navigate, and ultimately home.

[*screaming*]
[*static sputters*]

"*Emergency exit*: we have entered a time of general panic."[13] With no exit available at all, we exit into a state of permanent emergency. Panic as adrenal baseline, panic as mythic relation, panic as a metabolic state.[14] Panic as a *position*. "Panic has now become something mystical."[15] We carry it around in our pockets, thrumming and throbbing even in silent mode, vibrating as an extended apparatus of our very own bodies, the *entity* of ourselves as a collective subject, a parasitic alien mass *performing aliveness* as the subjectivity of a networked and predatory nervous system with no body at all—exoskeletal, lethal, and pristine. For it is not the world, per se, that is invoked by cosmic fear, but its double, its clone. The world has been removed and replaced by a cheap copy[16]—an emergency backup—simultaneously impersonating itself as its own terrifying Other. Cosmic fear as emergency reproduction. In which *this is not who we are* is indeed what we are. The total networked subjectivity of ourselves, en masse. The entity. The other us.

^o^

If by *The Day After* I was exposed, perhaps too early, to the ambient terror of a cosmic fear that could not be shaken, I was consequently able to discern three other modes of media-induced fear as a kind of taxonomy of cinematic terror:[17]

- <u>Narrative terror</u>: an absolute PTSD-inducing terror of narrative introduced by *When a Stranger Calls*, the 1979 domestic horror in which a babysitter's stalker is calling her from *inside the house,* delivering the devastating line on the home telephone: "*Have you checked the children?*"

- Aesthetic terror: a rapturous and disorienting aesthetic terror in the phantasmagoric unfurling of napalm ripping through the jungle and across a late-night television screening of *Apocalypse Now!* still branded into my visual cortex.

- Ontological terror: 1982. John Carpenter's legendary, *The Thing*, a film that must be seen to be *believed,* and otherwise requires no further ontological dissection, yet presages all morphing and devouring delirium to come—even by the mimicry of kitsch grotesquerie, right down to its final scene of two men stranded on the icecap not knowing if they or the other is human or imposter. The deepest ontological suspicion to the bone.

These are categories of convenience, to be sure, as most categories for understanding our encounters with art may be, but they bring us finally to David Lynch and his 2017 masterwork, *Gotta Light?* Part 8 of *Twin Peaks: The Return.* With *Gotta Light?* Lynch deploys all four modes of fear— narrative, aesthetic, ontological, and cosmic—as a unitary multiplicity of fears,[18] a synthesis that at every frame of timecode is greater and *never* the sum of its parts, neither wholly fictional nor verifiably real, but defying both form *and* the refuge of disbelief. There is no refuge from the Stockholm Syndrome of my own cinematic captivation. What Lynch summons in this integration of hybrid fears, unconstrained by a conventional demand for narrative payoff, is a suffusive Lynchian *intimacy,* that singular, unsettling *Lynchian fear* as its own category, invoked by infusing the existentially universal into the excruciatingly specific and idiosyncratically personal. Lynch famously generates that paradoxical intimacy here, in Part 8, by positioning *the bomb*, the world's first nuclear explosion—the Trinity Test—as its primary set piece, at the epicenter of the entire *Twin Peaks* narrative universe. And it is within the extra-narrative climate of a cosmic fear, out here, both symbolic and real, synchronous with a total melting-down of the media ecosystem in medium and content alike—and in their conflation as a *content device*—that Lynch deploys and ignites his own content device, that real epicenter upon which all things Lynchian converge, the Trinity Test.

Lynch's Trinity Test is an astonishing 2 minutes of illuminated historical reenactment, initiating a rapturous 10-minute work of video art, at the core a 57-minute masterpiece of avant-garde filmmaking, within an 18-hour episodically streaming movie—a production reportedly scripted, produced, and shot as a single film, then edited into a TV series, subsequently named by *Cahiers du Cinéma* the best *film* of the decade, that went on to screen in its entirety at the Museum of Modern Art—as the third season of a network television series at the culmination of a peerless career in American arthouse cinema.

Meltdown indeed.

Twenty-five years after *Twin Peaks* closed out a decade and sent us careening toward a new millennium, *Twin Peaks: The Return* excavates the origin story and temporal dysmorphia of that decade—the looping 1980s—looping back to haunt us: its Reaganomics, its feverish unreflected-upon nationalism, its *talk radio,* its ascendant NRA, its obsession with adolescence as a pornographic *tele-genesis*, and in this its cultural economy as social relation: the autonomic, self-engineering foundation laid for an entire country as a *social media* where a society might have been, the self-fulfilling prophecy of being devoured by the fiction of itself. What had been vaporized and unleashed at Trinity as an exchange of spirit and matter, turning us to ghosts and turning the desert to mirrored glass, had buried itself beneath *the mall* like the elephant's foot in the basement of Chernobyl and festered into a globulous goop of neoliberal lube, a glob of napalm bombing the indoor/outdoor carpeting of America as a sustained and savage assault by domestic disaster capitalism, the Kevlar fabric of *Americana,* had now finally returned in 2017 as the cost of the transaction. There are more civilian guns than people in the United States. Mass shootings, among them a horrific regularity of *school shootings,* have reached epidemic proportions. Drug overdoses ascended to the leading cause of death of Americans under fifty. An entire society committing capital suicide either by outright firing squad or by lethal self-medication—as *wellness* and *Thoughts & Prayers* fill the void of a universal health care, in the vacuum of society itself. HELL IS REAL. But it is not a place that can be atoned for. A real estate magnate, casino owner, and Reality TV star is president.[19] The Internet is reality. Reality is a doppelgänger. The 1980s are still looping as the genre-placeholder for the screaming alien future present. What is real is immaterial, liquid, ethereal, *unbelievable,* emergency, psychotic, perverse, horrific, or possibly not even happening at all. The call is always coming from inside the house now, though the landline has been severed. The aesthetic napalm is omnipresent. The ontological suspicion is intimately pervasive. The resulting cosmic fear is sustained. And *Twin Peaks: The Return* plays it by revelation—with Part 8 at its core, as the id of the ethos of the age: *Apocalypse.* And the apocalypse of apocalypse—a *native tourism* of apocalypse. What is seen through when there are no further veils to lift, but an endless procession of veils? In which it is easier to imagine the end of the world than it is to imagine the world[20]—the internal combustion of Trinity in this panopticon chamber blind, powering the engine of America.

^o^

The tracing of iconographic cairns inscribes a kind of psychic road map, even the most personal regional map, of a haunted America, an America haunted by its own paranormal present—its *presence.* A ghost map projected as the uncanny fabric of its own perpetually other self, a cinematic geography that can neither be located nor conveniently switched off. We don't get the art (or the artifact) that means what we want it to mean or that even means what it means. We get the art we deserve: the art we make. Virilio offers a desideratum of sorts to the contemporary experience. "The unprecedented aspect of what we are experiencing requires another way of thinking, a conceptual beyond, that I call *revelation,* in the apocalyptic sense of a *new day*."[21] An expansion of consciousness, which is a seeing and a willingness to see—the consciousness of our own inexorably shared experience. The holographic fabric of this cinematic real.

Minute 56 of Part 8 lands on what may be the most beautiful shot in the episode and possibly my favorite in the entire series—its final shot. The camera is fixed at the height of a man on a patch of desert ground at night, the New Mexico high desert roughshod with short scrub and rutted with tire tracks, sprawling briefly beyond a ring of electric streetlight and then disappearing into total darkness, neither north nor south nor east nor west, but vanishing into that exclusionary zone out there, inside the country. Abandoned waste, speculated real estate, hallowed ground. Lynch here is our Stalker, guiding us into the now that we're already so deeply, intractably inside. But to see into that Holocene murk, of a cinematic illumination. To see the light that sees and cannot see. Where is America?

Minutes 1–56

Minute 1

FIGURE 1 Twin Peaks: The Return © *Showtime 2017.*

It begins as it ends—with electricity. The *sound* of electricity. The *RR* production logo strobing inside the globe of an antique lightbulb filament against a black-and-white television sky, crackling with static electricity. *A Rancho Rosa Partnership Production* sizzling uninsulated at the intersection of raw power and illumination. Power and illumination, like lightning seeking ground, searching for form and location. And a bargain at the crossroads—that voodoo coordinate that is everywhere in America—our total encounter with that electrifying circuitry (Figure 1).

But for the adept, venturing the night-crossing. For the payment is not made simply with one's life. Only the living may pay their debts, and our debt, as ever, is the soul—that face of ourselves that is our encounter with the world, open to it as witness and devoured by it in exchange, as the suffering of that rapture, the sentience of the transaction in the symbolic field of real abstraction: the *art* of electricity. Lynchian electricity. Conducting souls.

A swelling bell tone sustained as angelic tinnitus, ringing in reverse: the tail end of a knell yet to clang. All sounds, as all things, are internal. A rainbow-rimmed lens flare passing over fog like a searchlight. A stand of dark trees breaking through the fog in the far right of the frame, trees we remember as the iconic Douglas firs of the North Cascades; and then *Laura's eye* appearing in the milky clearing of that probing light, the iconic portrait of Laura Palmer emerging briefly from the mist and then disappearing again. A slender bank of vertical sunlight cutting through the haze as the camera rises over the Boreal northwood and its river of fog; and rising with it, a swelling, cottony tension finally broken by the sighing daytime melodrama of a familiar Fender Rhodes electric piano: the opening notes of Angelo Badalamenti's effusive and melancholy theme, and the iconic corresponding title-over: TWIN PEAKS.

Twin Peaks in its signature *Avant Garde Gothic Condensed* font and two-toned putrid neon green, the hue of bile and mint acid, as radioactive *lettering*. The magical technology of the font itself is a total encapsulation, a prismatic, fractal expression of the whole. So potent is the *spell* of the iconographic *Twin Peaks* title that it improbably invokes an entire anthropocentric century of memetic branding from *Coca-Cola* to *Miami Vice* to *Apple* (et al., ad infinitum) and bears unexpected comparison once more to another juggernaut of world-building that has *returned* again and again over the past twenty-five years: *Star Wars*,[1] in which that imagined world is no longer represented as a *movie* at all (or even a sequel, or a sequel to a sequel) but is so vastly distributed across forms that it has become a *font*. A distillate elixir of meme. A migration-of-representation endemic to the times, in which *branding is narrative* and narrative itself assumes the structure of a font-as-living-meme, a *storytelling* (in industry content-speak) whereby *font is content* as a kind of fiberoptic, archival DNA.[2] No need to proceed further. In the case of *Star Wars,* it is enough to simply behold, at a glance, the self-advertising billboard of its iconographic font in order to receive the surface of its total contents. Or a *Coca-Cola*, which contains exactly what it says it contains—what it *means*—so precisely that the font *is* the effervescent sensation and elation of the taste.[3] *Twin Peaks,* on the other hand, compels us inward by a bit of false advertising, and in *The Return* this will become its outstanding feature: the disorienting, deimatic display of a vast and covertly coded system, concealed as daytime soap opera. A kind of fluorescent rune, signifying itself by the shimmering mirage of an enfolded misrepresentation, and in the resulting exhilaration triggered by an unreliable advertising: *we cannot know what this contains*. We have returned—but to where? To what?

Opening credits proceed, emerging and receding into the mist of Badalamenti's synthesizers. His theme is a remarkable achievement in musical scoring as sincere subversion, a soft siren swelling and swooning, soothing us to the shaggy carpeting of this experimental soap opera as a retroactive form of televised hypnosis, comforting and familiar. But something is different. A sense of time that has passed when we weren't looking. Or of time *missing*. The place is the same, but something is different. A drone shot floats us out over a rocky outcropping. We sense immediately that this aerial maneuver was not achieved with a camera mounted on a helicopter, but by something more disembodied. Drone. The fluid omniscience itself is signatory of the subjective *smoothing* of contemporary media. Here is the *Twin Peaks* we remember and recognize, but from an accessory point of view, as some kind of appendage to perception—a ghost prosthetic limb jarring in its polish and agility, portending that this is indeed 2017, not by what is seen, but already in the way of seeing. We look down upon the great rapids of Snoqualmie Falls pouring tumultuously out from under the

Great Northern Hotel, falling into the abyss, as if we are experiencing this gushing elemental catharsis, ever-flowing with torment to come, from the historic point of view of the Great Northern as an archival subject.[4] Or is it some other phantom perspective? Perhaps we are seeing from the subjective point of view of media itself.

Created by
Mark Frost
&
David Lynch

Minute 2

The misty backdrop of falling whitewater fades from aeration to the undulating blood-red of Lynch's signature curtains. Red velvet theatre curtains swaying fast with liquid agitation, faster than we remember them twenty-five years ago—another temporal modification of perception, as the proscenium to what lies beyond this suspension of disbelief is intensifying, quickening now with possession by some internal perturbation, a disturbance, an inflammation pulsating theatrical uterine space. The fourth wall is collapsing everywhere, with too many breaches to hold, crumbling all around us now and dissolving into the atomic pixels of total screen as totally lived encounter. Lynch's red curtains *performing* that funereal choreography of transformation, conducting us, enveloping us, enfolding us into Lynchian space on the threshold to a total dramaturgy of *Twin Peaks,* the land of the dreaming and the dead. Lynchian curtains flowing as the shape of Lynchian motion. By what agency? By which first cause is the cinematic space catalyzed and set in motion?

Already in the opening credits, we are oriented to Lynch's technique of isolating a specific vocabulary of cinematic artifice and theatrical props to abstract narrative effect—curtain, light, wind, fan, fire, smoke, dark, electricity—an established and recurring cast of elemental *characters* here as ambient and tactile as any human or dramatic device. By activating components of artifice with uncanny agency—observed in the hypnotic act of *moving themselves*—the viewer is conspired in the implication of an off-screen force, what photographers Cindy Sherman, Gregory Crewdson, Todd Hido, and Briscoe Park, or experimental filmmaker and video artist Eve Sussman embrace as *implied narrative*; in Lynch's case, a terrible, and terribly beautiful demiurgic force, forever remote but for the agency implied by its engineering as a cinematic effect. A counterfeit Logos moves about the room, inhabiting a cinematic fabric *between* the fictional narrative and the world, between its encoding and its revelation, migrating back and forth across the screen—the fourth wall itself as a phantom agency, exerting force upon the image at a spooky distance, conducting from the dark body of the world the encrypted messages we need to receive.

Directed by
David Lynch

Rippling red fabric fades to the iconic black-and-white lightning pattern of the *Twin Peaks* waiting room floor, a further activation of thematic set and setting. Lynch subverts his own aesthetic wheelhouse by disrupting the mid-century modern Americana of 1950s diner checkerboard tiles into its organic, perverse, and more dangerous field of symbolic electric current. The 1's and 0's of the binary chessboard and its ruthless algorithms of organization and strategic power are deranged into the alternating current of the lightning field. A floor ungrounded, warped, and volatile—the interior funhouse decorum of an elemental power of another order. Perception itself is divided in two, as the set piece chamber between the Black and White Lodges, the twin houses of good and evil that we may never access or perceive but for their representative mingling here as this perpetually threshold antechamber of multidirectional time. Perception of time is also divided into twos, as parallel currents running forward and backward, in stasis and in motion, sideways and as syrup, and as a *sentencing*, the aesthetic psychosis of *No Exit*, for as the final line of *The Return* will declare:[5] we can never abscond from time. We may only modify our own encounter with its attributes—alternately as Sisyphean, as Sartrean, as Beckettian, or as Kafkaesque as the room that we await to enter is the very room in which we wait. And this floor is spinning now, round and round as a record, faster and faster, until there is only its vertiginous turning beneath us, the flat circle of that time flowing away, turning back upon itself and fading to black and all music too.

Fade in on a frontal view of two men riding in a car at night. A hardboiled mood, skewed by the glossy saturation of video. What decade is this? Somewhere between 1970 and the interminable future present. Black and honey glow. Ragged reflections of overhead streetlights passing across the windshield, inserting a cinematic frame within the multivalent motion of the world. Ray Monroe (played by George Griffith) drives. Mr. C, or Bad Cooper (Dale Cooper's doppelgänger and one of at least three characters played by Kyle MacLachlan), rides shotgun. Mr. C withdraws a handheld device from the interior pocket of his black leather jacket. It's a cellphone, but in close-up the device displays a full-screen app in a simplified retro-futuristic style; not sci-fi exactly, but the sturdy matte brutalism of mid-1990s behind-the-curve futurism. Hardware. A kind of *Jason Bourne* tech-vibe briefly intruding into the Lynchian universe, the kind of temporal and aesthetic disorientation that will come to be defining of the series. Here, three black, rectangular, horizontal icons are anchored to a cerulean blue touchscreen, like Linktree click bars. Each of the three icons bears a symbol:

1. a pale green "C,"

2. a red "F I R E" (with cobalt blue triangles ornamenting both ends of the black rectangle),

3. and another pale green "D" and "X" separated by a white disc with a black dot center.[6]

The design effect of Mr. C's app icons is of coded-codes: a symbol system parallel and covert to our own lexicon of touchscreen symbols, shortcuts, emojis, emoticons, and the pantheon of branded and self-referential iconography at the fingertips of our shared visual cortex—familiar, yet indecipherable but to the agents of the ecosystem within which they have been transmitted. It's the briefest visual detail but results in the disorienting transformation of a universally recognized object (the cell phone) in an equally pedestrian and universal scene (the car ride), rendering what is so very familiar, contemporary, ubiquitous, and personal as being adjacent to our own recognition of it—suddenly conspiratorial, uncanny, and out-of-time. Everything we recognize is also estranged and rogue. The world we have designed has overtaken us, in the image of its collective engineer, a stranger.

Mr. C explains the meaning of the touchscreen icons by announcing to Ray that *"There are three tracking devices on this car."* His voice is a possession, an affectation by some other soul, deep and rich of body but dissociative, as though his trunk and head are being spoken by some other autism. He clicks off each of the icons and looks out through the windshield, instructing Ray to pull up close behind a box truck traveling just ahead of them. As Ray follows instructions, we finally see that they are traveling along what looks to be a divided suburban highway or mixed-rural county road. Mr. C keeps an eye on the cellphone device as Ray pulls right up behind the truck. The headlights of their car shine harshly on details of the truck's tail end: greasy folded-up liftgate, reflective caution-tape stickers, barn-door-style cargo doors, South Dakota license plate, and the bright lights of another car passing them in the oncoming lane. The banal composition of detail stands out as the "low production values" of a digital cinematography—or *television*—casting the scene in a Reality TV vernacular, at odds with the theatrical *unrealism* of the *Twin Peaks* universe, and setting us up to *catch ourselves* being repeatedly caught off-guard by our own dramaturgical expectations of fiction, of Lynch's highly stylized fiction, and above all, our expectations of *Twin Peaks*. But a signature strength of that stylization is the insinuation of Lynch's hand-crafted props into his scenes. The collision of Mr. C's handheld device, as a one-of-a-kind design object, with a pedestrian background captured in the pervasive digital populism of digital video, surreptitiously generates an entire aesthetic field: an ambient artifice (the customized device) suspended between an early 1990s anachronism of post-apocalyptic lost futurism and a *too-present* glaring kitsch realism (the Reality TV of the highway). *This Twin Peaks* is suddenly the found future present of a twenty-five-years-later-fictional-now. The effect is a destabilizing encounter with our own hybrid perception of now—*the ecstatic contemporary*—via the application of a radically interactive interface or the narrative conspiracy of a *reality device*.

If our own devices are an extension of each of our own bodies, networking us to electronic signals transmitted by a remote entity comprised of compound remote entities, then Mr. C's device is precisely that burner-appendage, prosthetic to an entity so far inside the dark interior of this *Twin Peaks* fiction that it may very well be outside it, out here.

Minute 3

Mr. C softly taps the license plate number of the box truck into his cellphone: **DEGWW8**. The predictive text function on the on-screen keyboard suggests DEFEAT and DEGAS as potential word choices, but he clicks the simple arrow icon signifying enter, and deflects his trackers onto the unsuspecting truck as a decoy. Force enacted at a spooky distance, again. The distance between the function of his device and ours. What is he? And from where or what *informing force* does he derive his signals? What are we—and what spooky constellation of ourselves informs us as that shadow entity, intimate and remote, human and inhuman?

"That should do it," he states impassively, then powers down the passenger-side window and tosses the phone out of the moving vehicle.

They ride on. Amber, dark and bright. The suburban highway is a thousand Midwest miles of off-world outpost night. From Toledo to oblivion. The end of the road repeating over and over and over again. There's a compression between them. Ray and Bad Cooper. A vast and terrifying loneliness sucked into the car from that vacuum of ozone, cosmic fear, and LED lights. Where once there was oxygen. We can never know each other again. We've been outsourced to some other purpose. The teleology of oil. A gazillion microbiotic souls led them to this. The blackened cave wall. Two animus figures sitting side-by-side in the automotive configuration of theatre seating, occupying that strange shared intimacy of forward-facing binocular, stereoscopic vision. Facing the screen. The same transparent screen that we are sharing with them. The two-way mirror, vulnerable to the predations of whatever entity may traverse the migration of that meta-viscosity, that conductive membrane translucent to *content*. There are many such scenes in *The Return*, in which their windshield is our screen—in landscape mode. A cinema of time travel, by going nowhere at all. The character is the viewer, emptied. There's no one there at all. The end of Muybridge at the end of America. When we've run out of geography, what happens then? All of this.

"*Where we going?*" asks Ray.

"*You'd probably like to go to that place they call The Farm.*" Mr. C suggests, as if putting thoughts in Ray's head.

"*That's what I was thinking.*" Ray replies.

Minute 4

Mr. C gets to the point. "*You have something I want, Ray.*"

"*Yes, I do,*" Ray confirms. "*I got it memorized. All the numbers . . . memorized perfectly.*"

Code again. Coordinates corresponding to an opaque place out there, behind the map of the world, a black site in the mind, inside the viewer, a blank spot between all things. And yet Ray attempts to situate that data within the scope of his own self-interest, as material leverage, as capital, the insult of real estate. *"But honestly, Mr. Cooper . . . I think it might be worth some money. Maybe . . . quite a lot of money."*

And from a side-angle setup outside the driver-side window, Mr. C turns his head slowly toward the camera to gaze upon Ray in profile, so that we are in his direct line of sight as he locks in on Ray. He doesn't blink, as if his eyes need never close.

"You think so, do you?"

It's a chilling gesture, the shortest path to exposing the vulnerability of Ray as he drives and the vulnerability of the viewer, riding along out here in the open field. In this single, controlled action we see things for what they are, even into that terrifying opacity withheld from us: that Agent Cooper is gone. In his place, now riding alongside Ray, is Mr. C—or Bad Cooper—one of Special Agent Dale Cooper's fraudulent doppelgängers. He has just been sprung from prison, a cell that could never contain him, and Cooper himself, among the most beloved, impossibly just, and Apollonian figures in all of dramatic history—a protagonist's protagonist—is nowhere to be found. Instead, he is buried deep within the interstices of the narrative itself, ensconced somewhere between the cathodes and off-screen gray matter of an encrypted and redacted backstory to which we are not given access. There is another currency in this world: the black market of dark time.

"What year is this?" Dale Cooper will ultimately ask, upon *his* eventual return. A question as conclusion, with the clock running out. Is it 1989?—in the very moment that Cooper was split into two, cleaved by courage and curiosity, his own openness to riddle and paradox—the moment that darkness caught up and entered him. Or is it 2016, when he time-traveled to meet Laura Palmer in the woods, just before her 1989 murder, altering the timeline forever? Or is it the year out here, in the digital night and quantum broad daylight, in the shared excruciation of this, the longest year, the year of forgery and of the forging of the replicant real—this extended, unending, and looping *year* of 2017, beneath the Great

American Eclipse[7] and the M87* black hole[8] when all errant pathos has come home to roost?

Or are 1989 and 2017 the same year?—the year that Laura Palmer and I were both high school seniors, and the glitching that the culture won't stop itching. Time has run out now, hasn't it? And it's happening again. For by its own narrative design, *Twin Peaks* is doppelgänger to the year itself, or whatever symbolic and hallucinatory unit of representation we may ascribe to this reality. There can be no thing without its other, without its copy in the series of itself as an infinite chain. Even the mountain of the world, twinned in the reflection of its antimatter. The distance between them is infinite, but *the 1 and the 0 = 2.*

^o^

In his first and only nonfiction essay, *The Kekulé Problem, Where did language come from?*—also synchronistically published in 2017[9]—Cormac McCarthy describes the phenomenon of language as that ontological revelation that *one thing can be another thing:* that the word for "water" *is water*; or *Coca-Cola* is a Coca-Cola; or *Twin Peaks is Twin Peaks.*[10] This technology of language as collapsible, portable, archival representation; a hyperobject with infinite surface area and zero mass; an extra-biological technology that spread like wildfire, defying geographical constraint and arriving recursively whole, perhaps as a kind of viral fractal, did so in the scant span of approximately 100,000 years ago, though its precise origins recede into anthropological darkness. But from it, all subsequent developments have rapidly emerged. The *unconscious*, on the other hand, which is predisposed to communicate in *pictures*, according to McCarthy, had been doing so quite effectively for *millions* of years, with no apparent need for language at all. Millions of years of pictures, of internal cinema, of nightmares, of dreams, and of the world. And then the *technology* of language. In which one thing can be another thing—in the transfusion of pictures into code, and then back again, with a lithium membrane wall of impossible viscosity between them. And we reside there—on that porous proscenium threshold of swaying red curtains and pixelated magma—as *agents*, at the liquid, glossolalic confluence of the cinematic unconscious and its extracorporeal technology of language.[11] McCarthy was a novelist, not a linguist, an anthropologist, or a psychologist, but his flight into nonfiction was worth it for a single sentence, among his best; a definition of the unconscious in his wry, signature style:

The unconscious is a machine for operating an animal.[12]

A machine inside each of us. Is it countless individual machines or one single machine? A shadow program, or background app—a *daemon*. And now that daemon is *outside* too. As the artificial sentience of language. Code. The machine for operating an animal has been released from its black box, exported, and networked at scale. Symbol and sign, signifier and signified, have merged into a kind of total VR hieroglyph—representing itself as a total doppelgänger and writing the scripts for itselves, for more of itself. Out here beneath the tsunami of image and meme, words and code, representation has overtaken the represented, overtaken the world. And language itself has taken on the lifelikeness of an *entity*, a performance entity *performing sentience*. Animal unconscious has turned itself inside out and been loosed upon the world as extravehicular. The walls of the cave are crawling, writhing with language. A post-human language entity. Language itself as a proto-AI, generating cosmic fear. "When God made man," McCarthy wrote in *Blood Meridian*, "the devil was at his elbow. A creature that can do anything. Make a machine. And a machine to make the machine. And evil that can run itself a thousand years, no need to tend it."[13] The machine for operating an animal has made a machine to make an unconscious machine. An operating animal, running in the silent whisper, in the cooling fans in the black. Running through us and running us through.

No need for speculation. Log on—as an army of Log Lady bots might say. It's all there. In the world, inside you now. The well of souls and those who are not souls, bleeding back and forth across the surrogate and the real; the cruelty of the one, the refuge of the other. From 0 to unwatchable. The recent digital work of Frank Manzano[14] is a kind of AI-generated Harmony Korine, morphing as horrific and mesmerizing suburban video grotesquerie. The effect is an abominable simultaneity of Gazan livestream and West Palm Beach *Grand Theft Auto*, as the neurological terror of contemporary experience, catastrophic and criminal, both online and off—as each other. Lynch intuitively reverse-engineers the disturbing physiological monstrosity of this algorithmic behaviorism and stuffs it into human bodies as characters with lines, acting out impersonal forces. *The Return* dramatizes this epic shadow-play of avatars, as a terminal origin story and radiant spectral field. From somewhere inside the forged and foul breath of a fraudulent Logos, it has generated the predatory machine of Bad Cooper as Mr. C.

Inside the moving vehicle, brazen in the illusory confidence of being behind the wheel and in possession of the numerical sequence that he has memorized as leverage, Ray has no notion of the non-negotiable malevolence sitting beside him. But in the dead weight of Mr. C's facial musculature, in the methodic *rotation* of his head upon a reptilian brainstem, in the unblinking gaze, and in our own forced positioning in his line of sight, we recognize the chilling *flat affect* of Hollywood's psychopathic lineage—from Norman Bates, Michael Myers, Jason, Hannibal Lector, and Buffalo Bill to *Se7en*'s John Doe and *American Psycho*'s Patrick Bateman; Schwarzenegger's *Terminator*[15] and especially *Blade Runner*'s iconic Roy Batty;[16] even *Alien*'s xenomorph and the now archetypal, impassive red eye of the HAL 9000.[17] For in *Twin Peaks*, characters are neither human nor inhuman; they're cinematic—ending here, at the windshield where the fourth wall of fiction meets the ongoing post-human now. The psychopath is at large, self-electrocuting into a flatline as the predatory flat effect of society itself—of us, the one we have engineered as that murderous para-worldly entity, the viral malware of the world corrupted and held hostage by an imposter forged in its own sociopathic image: a collective imposter syndrome, comprised of information, and of capital, coordinates, and code. The imposter is us.

And Kyle MacLachlan's performance of Dale Cooper as Mr. C is itself an act of hostage-taking, of one character by another, and of the audience held captive by a force inside the fiction exerting negative counter-force on the world. It's a performance gleaned through a Brechtian prism, a masterclass in alienation effect: a character honed against the audience's unfulfilled expectations of who we thought we needed this actor (and character) to be. Earlier, in Part 2, Mr. C would say to Ray (in a diner, of course), *"I don't need anything, Ray. If there's one thing you should know about me, Ray, it's that I don't need anything. I want. And I want that information."* That shuts Ray up fast. Ray believes that Bad Cooper is human, perhaps a damaged one. We suspect that he might be otherwise, a damaged copy. But there is no reason to doubt him when there is not a trace of doubt in his clinical introspection, his self-knowledge: *I don't need anything. I want.* A revelation of character in which subtext has been stated directly as text[18]—again, in this case, as sociopathic flat affect. The character is the text. There is no subtext. There is no character there at all. It's a chilling reversal. Conventionally, we understand inhuman predators (in this case a human *copy*) as having no desires, but only needs. Metabolism, protein, territory, reproduction. But Mr. C has no needs at all—only wants. He is invulnerable. He is not surviving, he is *choosing*. He is pure power of will. The absolute terror of absolute free will. Some kind of machine operating some kind of animal.

Consequently, the *absolute surface* of Kyle MacLachlan's Mr. C grows with time and repeated viewings as being remarkably adept—surprisingly complex, understatedly rich, and bone-chilling in the prescience of its specificity. There's something too of Anton Chigurh here, Javier Bardem's masterpiece of a twenty-first-century psychopath in the Coen brothers' film of McCarthy's *No Country for Old Men*. Chigurh and Mr. C are blood brothers of a new phenotype, an emergent and terrifying archetype: the psychopathic archetype, assembling out of discarded psychological scripts, scraped from the slopes of the uncanny valley itself like 3D-printed brimstone. The AI in human skin, the taxidermy of ourselves as inhuman algorithm—void of empathy. If Chigurh is the cruel administrator of probability and chance, the manifest agent of an absent God that *does* play dice, then Mr. C is the agent of that algorithm itself: the coordinates that locate that black code to its temporal blooming, the codex of black magic incorporated. In the end they are both but managerial operatives, as avatars of that absent god, that intelligence *forged*: the lethal and replicant emptiness of these times. *These times,* devoid of an Agent Cooper. Out here, inside this labyrinth of mirror and mirage, lost and drifting within a kind of animate cave painting of neurological peril and medication, when we needed him the most—to show us the way, to discern the true from the false, the original from the fake, the 1 from the 0 from the 2—Agent Cooper is gone. His absence is devastating. The great power of *The Return* is in what it has withheld. The arachnid photo of that black hole that it captures and shows us as evidence. We are on our own, abandoned in the void, left with ourselves to navigate this Black Lodge and the absolute dead of Mr. C's black eyes. Two black holes on the other side of this screen to which we have bound ourselves and into which we have stared, day in and day out, and kept staring. And now the black hole is staring back. Seeing what we see.

"You think so, do you?"

Mr. C turns away from Ray, away from the camera, away from us, facing forward to look out through the windshield again, moving through the night.

Minute 5

Ominous undertones as they roll along the expressway. Ambient white noise and the somnolent moaning of tires across asphalt smoothed suburban.

"There it is. Take that little road up there on the right. Let's get off this highway, Ray."

Ray follows instructions and pulls off the highway onto a curving exit ramp, the glare of black and yellow cautionary arrows reflecting in their headlights. Camera following their exact trajectory from the point of view of the car, just beyond the windshield. Attention heightened in the restricted field of vision. Organic tension is generated in the unembellished flow of action. We're watching, not what's happening exactly, but what hasn't happened yet. It's a tactic employed in setups for jump-scares. But here, tension, and its expected payoff as *fear*—as always with Lynch—is sustained as dread on the interior of the cinematic surface. A swelling in Badalamenti's score and Dean Hurley's sound design as the curve changes direction along an unfinished cinderblock wall and the road runs out of light. Now it's dark. A refrain Lynch's characters repeat across all his films. Dark, inside and out. Two wordless figures scarcely illuminated by the dim dashboard light.

Minute 6

Another tonal swelling as the road degrades to patches and ripples. Intimations of horror now in the headlights sweeping across a short stretch of rickety white fence rail rocked askew by the slow-motion earthquake of feral time. The interior of the car tremors briefly as it runs out of blacktop. Recollections of *Lost Highway* as our field of vision is reduced to a small pool of light skimming across an unmaintained dirt and gravel service road. More jarring inside the car as Ray follows the way. Badalamenti's soft minor mood is the narrative here, a plot of darkness probing: we really have no idea what's happening, no idea where they're going, no idea where any of this is going, and it's not clear that they do either. That's why we're here: *to not know.* Ray breaks the spell with another road movie line, of actors acting out road movie dialogue:

"You mind if I pull over for a sec? I gotta take a leak."

It's absurd, under the circumstances—that Lynchian strategy again, of erasing subtext for text, and inadvertently drawing peripheral attention to the plotless and unspeakable whole, foregrounding it by defying it, by stating the obvious, the pedestrian, the non-sequitur, or saying nothing at all. Of course Ray has something else in mind. But it's not *in his mind*. It's in whatever will follow. Psychology is not for Lynch's characters, it's for Lynch's audience.

"Go for it," allows Mr. C, in the baritone idiom of an equally absurd and macho banter. The idiom is *dialogue*. The story will move forward, or nowhere at all, whether we pander to it or not. Nowhere is there an attempt to simulate a dramatic realism. Instead, a cosmic narrative is activated in its antithesis: the cinema *of the audience*, vastly more expansive, interior, terrifying—and possibly more satisfying—than what we are trained to *believe*.

Ray slows down and stops in the dirt. It's our first omniscient perspective on the car, from a frontal, 3/4 angle, left to right: a rounded sedan, long and low in the cop cruiser style. *Car.* Narrow, viperine headlights consolidating all primary and practical source light about them. Video realism, smoothed and crude and brash. One shot and, we get the feeling, one take. Cinematographer Peter Deming and the Arri Amira digital documentary camera. But a psychology is not to be located in camera choreography either. *It is elsewhere.* It is rogue in the South Dakota midnight. Faint fill light, perhaps moonlight, trunk and rear window of the vehicle. A gorgeous natural palette in their immediate radius of night: prairie scrub grass and dust, maroon, and the edges of backlit green. No horizon. A well of ink. Or it's just not there at all. Ray gets out of the car, leaves the driver-side door open, crosses in front of the vehicle, and walks toward the camera.

Minute 7

Cut in to a medium shot of the car behind Ray, from the same angle and same point of view. It's the same shot but slightly closer, and Ray is now out of frame. A fundamental editing technique that Lynch and Deming and editor Duwayne Dunham repeatedly employ: establish the viewer's awareness of what falls within the total frame of a scene and then isolate one feature of the scene by quickly reducing our view of it within the frame. Ray, with his back turned just outside our own field of vision, cannot see what we see. Our point of view is precisely his blind spot: the interior of the vehicle completely consumed by darkness. Slight movement inside. The glove box opens. Empty and clean but for a handgun illuminated in the noir revelation of the glovebox bulb light. A panel of needlepoint blues glowing from the dashboard instrument lights. Mr. C withdraws the revolver and checks the cylinder. Beautiful resolution of detail in the leathery tone and shadow, the sinuous power of his hands, the confirmation of bullets in their chambers, firing pins and caps, and the weight of brass. A tactile sequence of objects in action, at the pace of objects, a psychology (finally now) of framing without ceremony, of what is seen and not seen, on screen and off, all confined within the front seat-space of a parked automobile. A radical contrast to the Hollywood velocity of action, or the *action of action*—a sublimating action, saturating the viewer in content in order to devour the viewer *as* content. Here we are cued into the awareness of ourselves taking stock of a forensic action as an orienting function of the frame. We are watching. If we are bored, we will either flee and alleviate that boredom, or we will sustain an attention to attention as its own kind of ecstatic awareness. We are watching. Mr. C gets out of the car, passenger-side of the vehicle, and stands, armed now, in near total darkness, facing Ray at the same angle where we now intuitively know that Ray is standing off-screen—

"Ray. I want that information."

Once again: bald-faced defiance of industry *storytelling*—of good screenwriting. Bad Cooper drives the scene by stating exactly what he wants, as an avatar—as an *actor.* The character himself is an actor here, with zero subtext at all, inhabiting that special place in hell for daytime drama night scenes. The contrivance, of course, is the soap opera as Lynchian artifice. A kind of narrative decoy (or red herring in the percolator), as if the real story is elsewhere. But where?

In the next shot, Ray is included in the frame. He turns around holding a gun of his own, though we can barely see anything at all, and Mr. C opens fire on him. But all he gets are the impotent clicks of a rigged gun—perhaps a *prop* gun.

"Tricked you, fucker."

Ray narrates his own action, repeating what the scene has already told us and doubling it now as blunt exposition with a Brechtian flourish of stating the obvious: that Mr. C is a *fucker.* Bad Cooper is characterized *by bad dialogue* and explicitly narrated action. *"Tricked you,"* he declares. It will happen again and again, because the story is elsewhere, in the interstices of a broken and syncopated surface, accumulating as the total *negation* of that sum of its parts—as alienation effect: the default vulnerability of our own rhythmic expectations as an agent of complicity in Lynch's alchemical project. Our experience of that alchemy is a spectacular synthesis of the hypnotic and the repellent, a manipulation that is not achieved by narrative cleverness but by an artful discontinuity, a reverent specificity to the discordant gears of his own visual narrative catalyzed by relentelssly undermining the cleverness of meeting narrative expectations.

Lynch is anything but a *clever* filmmaker, nor *tricky,* as Cassavetes might say. In the pursuit of a cinematic human truth, a radical emotional realism, John Cassavetes despised the clever and the tricky. As a fellow giant in American independent cinema, Lynch is something of Cassavetes' underworld antithesis, a mirroring in the canon on extreme sides of a Reality simulacrum. Lynch's pursuit is not toward a surrealism anymore than Cassavetes sought a contrived naturalism, but an upholding of the image and the scene which is true to the artfulness of itself and nothing else. The narrative architecture then is an exploded whole, not clever, but *present* with the profound idiosyncrasy of the painted surface as an inscrutable simultaneity with its interior. The surface is its interior, doubled as the *secret agency* of my own occult interiority—mysterious, oceanic, superstitious, unreliable, but also interrupting and behaving right upon the face of it. I am here too, as part of that exploded whole, as I am likewise the empathetic subject of Cassavetes' shared emotional naturalism; a cinematic witness to our own pathos and vulnerability, Lynch's anti-story shared darkly. And that anti-story is coming now, coming on fast.

Outside the vehicle, Ray opens fire on Mr. C and drops him to the ground with two shots to the gut.

Minute 8

Ray approaches Mr. C to see him lying on his back, unconscious. Then a reverse angle, looking up at Ray from just over and above Mr. C's shoulder. Ray raises his gun to put a few more bullets in the body for good measure, but he is interrupted by a flashing light. The ground pulsates with illumination like a flashbulb screwed into some great socket in the night. The soft prairie dirt is pitted with the hoof prints of some trampling western herd, longer scrub grasses dry and wild, and standing rocks, and a wallow shelter tree strobing brightly blue and silver halide in the paranormal heat lightning all around them. An apparition of figures coming out of the darkness. They move quickly toward the camera at a loping gait, an obscure number of strange and bearded men appearing as an otherworldly pack of desert derelicts and coal-car hobos blackened of the mines and filthy with coal-fired dust who seem not to have emerged from the chiaroscuro landscape at all but from another layer of celluloid altogether, simultaneous to the one occupied by Ray and Mr. C. They mob before Ray as a silent murder of crows, flagellating *transparently* about him in the black, and then they gather about Mr. C's body on the ground to commence with their crow funeral. Three of them— or is it five? or six?—in overlapping temporal transparency, with heavy coats and woolen hats and long wooly beards, they kneel and search and knead at the torso of Bad Cooper in a

FIGURE 2 Twin Peaks: The Return © *Showtime* 2017.

bewildering laying on of hands, probing and stroking his face roughly as animals despairing over their dead in some frenzy of voodoo first-aid as Ray, paralyzed and stupefied and standing there, looks on and inside and through these phantom men. A few muted tones culled from the longest strings of a piano or some other source.

Minute 9

And they are jumping, these bearded, soot-covered men. *Jumping around.* We've seen this before in *Twin Peaks*—in the cryptic Jumping Man, and Pierre, the grandson of Mrs. Chalfont/Tremond—each of them jumping as an expressive ambiguity falling somewhere between dance and ceremony, communication and physical gibberish, which can only be described as a kind of mute urgency, prelinguistic and nerved. How quickly Lynch cuts to the disorientation of truly not knowing what something means—which is why *uncanny* is over and over again so precisely used to describe his compositions. Yet it is by repetition that gibberish becomes sign and code, and vice versa: that something intelligible is rendered absurd—a theatrical language in which the artistry is the narrative, the production and post-production design exerting force on that narrative as much as any mapping of plot or written characterization, as a kind of haunted, radioactive matter interior to the total artwork. *Jumping, in a way that is wrong.* The visual disorientation and sinister vibe of this lawless ritual choreography are amplified by a minimalist ambient score, the dampened swelling and howling of undertones as though softly thumping from the underside of some remote and sunken hull, the surface of our own infected eardrum. The nightmarish soundscape here is allegedly a radically slowed-down recording of Beethoven's *Moonlight Sonata* laced with errant monkey screeches. As is often the case with Lynch, we are seeing and hearing something that we have never seen or heard before.

The feral men are jumping, and they are patting and pulling from Bad Cooper's torso lying on the ground, rooting around the body in the slowly strobing blue light until his face and white t-shirt are smeared with his own blood. They raise the lifeless head and hold the deadweight of him in their hands, moving it about as though he were undead and might be returned to them in their primitive encounter with the inexplicably dead. Ray flashes among them, lain over beneath the cross-dissolving gelatin transparencies. He too has fallen to the ground, grimacing in horror and slowly crab-crawling away, his own howls of disgust slowed down and muffled as the pained and toothless groaning of cattle giving birth to a demonic sonic fabric of the night.

Minute 10

But he sees it too, in the black and glistening black blood— some kind of black orb, a scorched volcanic egg sac engorged and tumorous, hemorrhaging from Bad Cooper's chest wound. Pulling in and centering on the vascular, amniotic balloon, a human face appears as an internal superimposition on the gore: the demonic, smiling face of Bob, the *Twin Peaks* archetypal face of pain, torment, and evil, now alarmingly bulging and grinning from the chest cavity of Mr. C as a parasitic organism. It is a shocking (and disgusting) reverse migration of substance into form, in which trauma has manifested as its symbolic material form. If unthinkable *evil* had been anthropomorphized as the fiendish and menacing demon *Bob*, chronically stalking Laura Palmer from within the safety of her own teenage bedroom, we now encounter that disembodied force of action in his visceral and incubated state. Where once Bob had inhabited Laura's father, Leland, as *symbolic* of his own terrible deeds—as the unthinkable cause and mutual denial of those deeds—Bob is now the face of evil as morphological autonomy, a haunting of physiology itself, in which the traumatic consequences of profoundly damaging behavior—in this case rape and incest and murder—are capable of crossing the blood-brain barrier as a kind of malignant orgone. Lynchian ontology recapitulating Lynchian phylogeny. Dramatic spirit as grotesque existential physiology. *Bob*—is simultaneously symptom and underlying cause; simultaneous cause and affect, where none can be atoned for. A trauma so profound that a disruption of *temporality* is the only way around the truth, as blank spots on the map of time. The map of memory. That the world as it is cannot be looked upon, is not there at all. That the world is not capable of suffering the truth of itself. That there are truths too painfully unreal to bear. And for this accretes fiction, the wave cancellation of the unreal as unreal—or the art of resolving paradox with excruciating ambiguity, where all others fail. The conspiracy of fiction, where reality cannot be looked upon and which charts its own history.

When Bob was exorcised by Leland's suicide, in the conscious light of his own horrendous act of filicide, he required a new host. He found one in the single weakness of Special Agent Dale Cooper—the Good Cooper: in the hubris of having no fear, of entering the Black Lodge waiting room willingly, the crucible of that temporal disruption, and confronting its irreconcilable truth. The conspiracy of the narrative itself. The conspiracy that a unified field theory of *Twin Peaks* is always beyond our grasp. A skeleton key forever out of reach, forever incomplete.

That there is no proof. The black box is sealed, as it is, in the theatre inside the television transparent and humming of shifting sooths, as woodgrain and clouds and rainbows in gasoline. Cooper watching it. And us watching Cooper watching. Searching it—looping. Altering the position of the particle and the wave by the very act of his own observation, himself the conspiracist in the end, the conspiracy of the crime. Of things that can never be themselves. For the one and the zero are two. So Bob entered the doppelgänger of Cooper as a *corruption* in the splitting of the light, and Cooper overtook himself in the curtains of that atom-splitting night. Bob occupies the evil deeds of men, and the men who would commit evil deeds, in the psychological space of *real* terror. And we will soon learn of his true origin in the chain of that *symbolic real*—generated by the banality of cosmic evil and the opportunity generated by its cosmic fear: the vacuum of spectral real estate that evil rushes in to occupy in order to prey on the vulnerability of real people.

The phantom horde of Woodsmen have been roused from interstitial night by the felling of that imposter, and rushed in to tend to the incubus adult-infant infested inside, some kind of awful fetal co-habitation nursed now from the guts of Bad Cooper in this emergency cesarian opera, still strobing over a horrified Ray Monroe. And Ray has seen enough. So he is disappeared from the shot, tearing across the front grill and narrow serpent-like headlights of his sedan parked in the country dirt, all sandy gold but so drained of color that everything reads as blue. Ray slips and falls at the right front corner of the car, again disappearing from view, and scrambles along the far side of the automobile. The driver-side door is flung open, and then slammed shut. It's a micro-action escape sequence in which we hardly see Ray's body in motion at all. Another cut-in to the car as he spins the tires and speeds away; the same shot but slightly closer, so that the tires are out of frame—a subtle but adept narrative edit for such experimental work—and then Ray is gone, tearing through a mirage of menacing Woodsmen and leaving only dust behind: a frame of smoke billowing on the black and blue night. The Woodsmen continue their odd, jumping, circular dance from the blown-up POV of the camera itself, so that all we see are the incomplete gestures of their over-coated, mongering forms in the moonlight, on the simulated surface of celluloid. And then darkness. A muted earthen murmur and soft wash of static as sand flowing through an hourglass, and nothing but smoke, a scrim of dust hanging in the strobing blue light. And then darkness again. A long darkness.

Minute 11

Dust hanging there, moving in the air as a curtain of smoke. Ambience and aftermath as theatrical objects themselves. Lynch hypnotizing in the ease and fearlessness of his gifts as a painterly filmmaker, and foreshadowing the peripheral array of our nervous systems that will be required by the path to come. And then a limbic pause. Attention on our own attention. A full eighteen seconds of near black. And the slightest modulation in pitch of white noise.

A reticent moon, cornered as a spider's egg, glowing gothic and inward upon a frame's worth of night-racing clouds. The last witness of opacity unto opacity. Ray too, racing through that noir, his cheekbone and jawline, the oval of his face itself a small moon above the arc of the sedan's steering wheel. The pale glow of a cell phone held on-speaker and he urgently dictating his whereabouts as he drives, the strange things he thinks he has seen, and what they might mean. The racing lines of the road angled as chalk-drawn daggers toward the diminished horizon, infinite in the blind pitch blackout beyond, that lost highway itself our own inscribed field of vision. And he's talking to Philip, leaving a message for Special Agent Philip Jeffries—once played to astonishing effect by the great David Bowie—embedded somewhere out there on the other end of that message, in the backwaters of this cosmic statecraft, where the semiotics of power and voodoo are interchangeable in the maintenance of all events unfolding as a dark flower in the blacklight, in the conspiracy of the encrypted night.

Minute 12

Hard cut to a medium close-up on those very *instruments* of voodoo, shimmering in the iridescent metal of a scarab's carapace. A band of musicians swaying as venomous seaweed inside that rippling foil of aquarium light. A singer slung behind a killer's black shades, coiled in predatory repose against the slant and silver firing pin of a mic stand, and a wraith rumbling through it as some harsh and scraping wind shearing down the face of a sonic avalanche glitching in place, gravel ground and grating by the chronologic machinery of some wiry beast roaming this spectral plain where geology is the theatre of nightmare.

Cut now to a tuxedoed announcer standing before a microphone adorned with a *pinecone*. If the world has produced a more perfect shape of itself, then I don't know what it is or if we would recognize it. There's a sadness in the emcee's eyes, a distance of solemnity, and a brightness too, but some sadness enveloping.

"Ladies and Gentlemen, The Roadhouse is proud to welcome—"

Played by the actor J. R. Starr, the role of the Roadhouse MC is recurring throughout the eighteen episodes of the season as the announcer of each Roadhouse musical guest; a unique structural attribute of *The Return*, each episode featuring a live musical performance, and all but this one—Part 8—arriving at the end of every episode, further blurring the distinction here between a theatrical reality and a cinematic fiction, and of what's to come in the minutes ahead. The appearance of Starr as the MC in each episode is brief, but striking. In his black-tie tuxedo, he joins the ranks of other dream-state attendants to the White Lodge—the Giant, the Fireman, the elderly waiter in the Great Northern Hotel, and the timeless waiting room crooner, Little Jimmy Scott. Starr is also, along with Scott, one of the very few Black actors in the entire *Twin Peaks* universe, both of them portraying showmen, or ferrymen to a theatrical dream state.

Lynch has been criticized (alongside his recurring depictions of disturbing, misogynistic violence) for casting non-white actors in roles that are secondary and freakish, or otherwise exoticizing characters of color at the periphery of a core white cast. It is an observation not entirely at odds with a melodrama unfolding in the late 1980s in the rural Pacific Northwest, surreal and nightmarish as it may be, but one that endured as a flashpoint issue in the turbulence of 2017 into which *Twin Peaks* made its return; a criticism highlighted by an internal geography expanded well beyond backwoods Washington State, into South Dakota, Las Vegas, Texas, and even New York City; and a *Twin Peaks* further expanded into a narrative and media climate characterized by hyper-vigilant awareness surrounding representation, across a networked climate of *weaponized awareness of awareness*. Critic Frank Guan assessed the compound issue in his excellent and compelling essay for *Vulture*, *What Does David Lynch Have to Say About Race?* In an expansive consideration of Lynch's entire body of work, Guan asks directly, "What does David Lynch, one of the most (if not the most) important artists white America's produced in the postwar era, have to say about race?" It's a legitimate interrogation to make of an artist of such monumental cultural stature, even if that examination is undermined by the nature of the medium itself: the tenacious ambiguity and contextual inter-subjectivity of art-making by design. Guan's insights are adept:

The fall of Cooper, the character closest to a Lynch self-portrait, cuts to the heart of his signature achievement as an artist. He has converted, by force if necessary, white America's simplistic, innocent vision of itself into a complex and incendiary demonology. There has always been a latent contradiction in the phrase "American Dream." Dreams are the foundation of memories and the house of conscience, but more often than not the success (linked invariably to the possession of white skin) that defines the American Dream demands the forfeiture of memories and conscience. Lynch's works live in that contradiction and enact its inevitable bad consequence. A society founded on amoral, amnesiac legends of success cannot help but be poisonous: If his art is not an antidote (art is not an antidote for social ills), it is the next best thing, a mirror in which the act of poisoning is faithfully reflected, a toxicology report.[19]

Art as toxicology report. And all of Lynch's art is a kind of cinematic drawer filled with forensic evidence from some ambient crime scene—of a society that *sees itself as cinema via cinema*[20]—the American trauma-cinema: that uniquely American *cinematic consciousness of itself as a sacrificial* society, a society that positions itself within the living psychic framework of an apocalyptic survivalism, and has outsourced that survivalism to the voodoo of *Thoughts & Prayers*. But that trauma-cinema of the American Dream is also the hypnotic, perilous, gangrenous, and candy-coated, radioactive garden in which Lynch luxuriates and sculpts his visions, and his visions of *evil* coiling and slithering therein. For it is not evil that has corrupted that garden, but a chain of corruption extending beyond the temporal horizon that allows evil to enter over and over again, in all its human and parahuman forms. It is *systems* that generate encounters so inhumane, impersonal, antipathetic, cruel, merciless, and destructive that they are described as an abstract force of evil—even within the system of an individual, whose attitude and actions may be so heinous that they are only attributable to supra-individual contexts of environment, socialization, education, chemistry, genetics, nature, mass psychology, politics, and political economy[21]— in which *individuals are not themselves.* It is the encrypted metadata of that systemic force to which Lynch gives us access, as a semiotics which is indecipherable beyond the form it has taken. It stands for what it is, symbolic of its own meaning, beyond which lie only more meanings animately encrypted as themselves in a chain of radically ambiguous and menacingly unstable forms descending into opacity, as the cinema of an infinite tarot deck extending over the event horizon.

Lynch's forms—his *castings*—are not accuracies (or corrections), but specificities (and damages) as that menacing instability; those *forces* of evil and the ultimate failure of intention to maintain integrity in the face of it. The system is flooded with the counter-valency of those opposing intentions, transforming and deforming and electrifying, and that hot contact is the animating force of his scenes and their encryption as scrambled signals—the engine of mystery, threat, and captivation. In truth, *all* of Lynch's characters are subject to absurd levels of idiosyncrasy, hyperbolic freakishness, and the broad brushstrokes of performative, stereotypical characterization—a *theatricality* rarely falling inside the constraints of believability or naturalism and often in equal measure to an environment characterized by an *absurdity of banality,* and traumatic levels of that sustained banal/absurd circuitry. Each of his characters witnesses that circuitry from somewhere on the networked skein, at risk of being destroyed by it—providing alternate ways of seeing, speaking, coding, decoding, comprehending, and atoning; alternate maps and means of navigating the electrified field of picket fences so prone to electrocuting all who come into contact with it: the world as it is, generated by an alternating current of dream and nightmare and with scant solid ground of a *real* to be found. When what is most desired—most needed—is safety, here upon a geography of hot-wired pathos and illumination there is no such insulation within which to seek refuge.

It is the divergent, the psychotic, the psychedelic, the paranormal, the clairvoyant, the mystic, the obsessed, the neurotic, the mentally unwell, the isolated, the shut-in, the outcast, the addict, the seer, the mute, the bereaved, the tormented, the soulful, the mystic, the Tibetan (method), the indigenous, the astrologist, the cosmonaut, the carny, the criminal, the freak, the hort, the dream being, the angel, the poet, the double (even of oneself), and one widowed Log Lady *signing* the pain and the poem of the encrypted way—anyone and everyone but the executioner's binary reason, its denominated mean, and the repressed savagery of its anemic culture-less culture, its algorithmic lawn, its gated electric fences, and its martial identity cosplay providing the inevitable private security necessary for a sustained implementation of domestic disaster capitalism: *a society as weaponized real estate*, in which there is finally no refuge anywhere. *All of space infected* by the extreme logical conclusion of private property as ethos: the elimination of space itself by the total infection of total real estate—the air we breathe, the water we drink, the images we see, the messages we send, the thoughts we think—reality itself captured and *possessed* as infected content. Reality as doppelgänger to itself, an imposter singularity of content, a black hole of content; and the imminent collapse of geography into that black hole of content, both symbolically and actually; and with it the wildwood frontiers of the unconscious, collapsed and closed, harvested and burning— the rogue denizens of that flickering hinterland panicked and scattered and fleeing as roaches with nowhere else to go, demanding quarter *inside* the house, and with them all dark forces lamprey to the streaming migration.

In Part 8, Lynch illuminates the total televisual syndicate of that criminal system by linking directly Laura Palmer's horrendous violation and the destruction of her family to a *time bomb* buried at the core of the culture—the engine of a cosmic fear and chronic state of cosmic psychosis, a social psychosis as shared temporal dissociation: a symbolic field in which the moment-by-moment possibility of instantaneous self-incineration *means* that absolutely *nothing* can be trusted, from the grandest scale of transnational commerce and infrastructure to each and every pixel of atomic composition. Again and again—a conspiracy in the timecode of reality itself. All is compromised. Above all, the protagonists of the corrupted artifice, the symbolic crux of the fraudulent cultural economy, the high school of America and its permanent teenage avatars of a collective id throbbing and bursting like neurons inside the great strobing and smoking TV of America. It is the iconic sacrificial prom queen, her nuclear family, and a Special Agent of the FBI[22] who ultimately suffer the spiritual corrosion of that deeply internal corruption: the *Twin Peaks* quartet of Laura, Leland, Sarah, and Dale as the *antagonist protagonists* of a vast narrative conspiracy, the personified branding of American social architecture demolished in anguish, violent transgression, self-destruction, and temporal disintegration verging on nostalgia psychosis.

"The year is 2017," Guan concludes in his critical essay for *Vulture*, inadvertently answering Cooper's fugue-state question in the final moments of the series. "However you look at it or feel about it, the American Dream as we've known it is on its way out, and no one can be sure what or how much will survive its termination."[23] On its way out—or involuting, transfiguring, and blooming like blacklight mold into a phantasmagoric field of shared, personal hallucinations. The archival pathos of the American Dream that Lynch will conduct now in Part 8, in the sprawling minutes to come—deranged, violent, shining, and sublime in its perpetually mythic genesis—is the cinematic document of that dreamer seeing itself for the pastoral monster that it is, in that temporal geography melted into mirror. The nightmare of the dreamer dreaming. Hemorrhaging through the cracked veneer of Hollywood homecoming and country club sheen, pooling as motor oil in the streetlight, the blood of the malevolent entity. The machine that makes the machine and runs a thousand years. In the weaponized gibberish of a corrupted script. Even Cooper could not rewrite it, could not fix it, could not make it right, *could not remember,* and could not return to his own right self. So it is pieces. Broken and incomplete and weeping. And that is its possibility. That there is anything out there at all. An owl in the night. Cleaving the darkness and the glaring commercial daylight.

^o^

It was in that glaring daylight on an afternoon in 1999 that I met the arm. We met on Sunset Blvd. There is no place on earth with quite the rhythmic ring of *Sunset Boulevard*. I was newly living in Hollywood and trying my hand at the business. I drove out there alone, across the desert, all the way from Ohio. I was delivering *diets* in Los Angeles to make ends meet when I glanced in my rearview mirror and saw a vehicle weaving in and out of traffic, barreling toward me from another place. What pulled up next to me at the stoplight was a ratty beige Chrysler LeBaron convertible with the paint peeling off and the ragtop up in the blazing Southern California sunlight. And sitting behind the wheel was the arm, the unforgettable dwarf impresario of the *Twin Peaks* waiting room, played in reverse by actor Michael J. Anderson. I was not prone to bugging celebrities. Hollywood is crawling with them. But this was not like meeting a celebrity, or an actor, or an artist, or even a person at all, but like meeting the artwork itself, the apparition of an otherworldly being. *The man from another place.* So with all due respect to the human at the center of all that projection, I made an exception. Besides, he was wearing yellow hunting glasses, like Hunter S. Thompson. I had no idea what to say, so I just leaned over and rolled down my passenger-side window and shouted across the lane, *"You were the arm in Twin Peaks!"*

"*That's right!*" He shouted back.

"*I'm sorry to bother you,*" I said. "*I just wanted to tell you that I love your work. I love what you did with David Lynch.*"

"*Thank you,*" he said. "*David is the best.*" And then, in a backwards-sounding voice, he added, "*He is like Picasso!*" and snapped his fingers like the arm and squealed his tires and took off. Jackpot. I wasn't out there with anything to lose, so I took off after him and caught up at the next stoplight. Sunset

Boulevard, red lights all the way down, right when you need them.

"*What are you working on now?*" I asked.

"*We just finished a pilot. But I don't know if it's gonna get picked up.*" I couldn't know it at the time, but it was *Mulholland Drive.*

"*Who is his casting director?*" I ventured.

"*Johanna Ray.*"

"*Thank you!*"

"*No problem!*"

And then something extraordinary happened.

"*Hey—Maybe there's gonna be a party tonight. Some people will probably be there. Give me your number. I can let you know.*"

The arm wanted my phone number. *The arm* was inviting me to some kind of David Lynch party in Hollywood. *The arm was going to call me on the telephone.* I rooted around in my car and found a book of matches and a pen and furiously wrote down my number as legibly as I could and flung the matchbook out the window from between my fingers like a tiny frisbee, and it spun through the air between cars and hit the arm right between the eyes between the yellow lenses of his hunting glasses. "*Eureka!*" he exclaimed, and then tore off down the road to a meeting or to some other place. I went straight home and waited by the phone. I imagined the night ahead of me. The night and all its portals, the jacarandas in the purple night. The phone never rang. Somehow he was already inside my house, answering it. I didn't last long in Hollywood. It is a strange and lonely place. But I loved driving the megacity freeways at night, and that single encounter made every excruciating moment of isolation worth it. It was no big break. It was a Hollywood *breakthrough*—some kind of liquid rupture from one dimension into another. Beyond the calcified wall of an engineered irreality, there was an opening onto the banality of the otherworldly. Reality is alive in the extraordinary quality of things just as they are. A shitty mid-1990s Chrysler LeBaron on the trashy-ass Sunset Strip. All things were possible and coincident to labor and hustle and luck, anxiety and malaise, exhilarant in the diffusion of a strangeness into the world. A kind of void of faith. The waiting room is an electric, magical place.

^o^

Twenty-five years before J. R. Starr would announce the Roadhouse musical guest in minute 12 of Part 8 of *The Return*, Little Jimmy Scott, Ohio's own idiosyncratic, mid-century crooner, would electrify the final episode of *Twin Peaks* Season 2 with his ecstatic blues lament *Sycamore Trees,* a vocal performance of such intensity and sensitivity that it was nearly unbearable. A blues requiem staged dreamlike in the red-curtained waiting room, *Sycamore Trees* inscribed a circle of tender but searing illumination, a literal spotlight on pain, beauty, and loss as being inextricably intertwined. In his sublime, unearthly voice, Jimmy Scott summoned rare vulnerability into a devastating hymnal for the memorial moment, anticipating the possession and corruption of Cooper. It was Lynch at his finest, conducting a transcendental and indestructible sorrow running through the fabric of all things, a *sadness* that he has named often and directly, and as critic David Hering has written of *The Return*, that "from death there comes beauty, but the beauty is never inextricable from the source of death. The undertow of this enmeshment is a deep, deep sadness that suffuses everything, one that runs through the entire work."[24]

That boundless, inexhaustible sorrow was perhaps the single orienting experience of a soul—the soul of the viewer— passing through the otherwise radically disorienting and purgatorial antechamber to the Black and White Lodges, the dyadic, hidden houses of good and evil that we may never enter nor see but are interwoven as each other and intermingling as our own entertained perception of them *as* the curtained waiting room: in which the waiting room *is* simultaneously the Black Lodge itself, as the alternating current of interminable disorientation between the Black and White Lodges. There we encounter a syrupy temporal viscosity suspended between heightened attention and agitation—so heightened that we can hear a ring drop or the muffled reverse shuffle of soles across the floor—captivated by a magician's redirection of that great river of sorrow into the utter thrill of experiencing something that a television audience had never experienced before. *Sorrow and wonder.* And the current of sorrow can be reversed perhaps by the showman alone. The shaman as showman[25]—conducting us over the threshold to a transformative theatrical space where things seen are not possible, and yet are. There are no secondary roles in *Twin Peaks,* only players on either side of the curtain. In an extra-dimensional 1989, *the man from another place* (or the arm) and Little Jimmy Scott incanted us into the astounding artistry and temporal autonomous zone of the red-curtained waiting room. Twenty-five years later, J. R. Starr's MC is now the moment's witness, a master of ceremonies seeing us through the fraudulent fourth wall and initiating our descent into the suffusing source of an incendiary mythic real—the combusting epicenter of the American Dream so blinding that it is not possible to look upon, and yet is.

"Ladies and Gentlemen, The Roadhouse is proud to welcome the Nine Inch Nails."

A 4/4 beat commences crude and rude on the drum kit—primitive, summoning, and warlike. Shards and louvers of zinc and gunmetal light cutting across the pale faces and gothic skins of the band. A thuggish and soggy baseline lumbers back and forth between a whole step and the root like a doomsaying EKG-reading. Reverse angle on the blue and amber chiaroscuro of a packed house, the audience absorbed and swaying, all shoe-gaze and head-bang rave. Then Reznor throttles the mic stand like a crowbar, prying at the seam between stage and screen:

You dig in places 'til your fingers bleed
Spread the infection where you spill your seed

Minute 13

The guitar player abrades his electric strings in a frenzy of modal shriek, a musicality more machine-shop drill-press than human-made melody. Trent Reznor and his NIN (hailing also from Jimmy Scott's native Cleveland) telegraph all the agitation, alienation, and unsettling machine aesthetic of a disaffected Rust Belt grievance—post-industrial meltdown as the fraudulent veneer and neuropathic dissonance of the cultural economy itself *defecting* into psychotic bewilderment.

I can't remember what she came here for
I can't remember much of anything anymore

Minute 14

The irruptive appearance of Nine Inch Nails here at minute 14 is at once anachronistic and nostalgia-smashing: an apparition from the late 1980s origin period of *Twin Peaks* and a parallel cultural phenomenon, now re-contextualized *inside Twin Peaks* as an abrasive and dissonant oracle of the disc-skipping future present, a glitching of the permanently contemporary, devoid of future. The live performance of the *real* industrial band inside the *fiction* of *Twin Peaks* is fourth wall-disrupting, or fiction-disrupting. And here Trent Reznor inhabits a mercurial role upon this Roadhouse stage, in which he is neither exactly a character in *Twin Peaks* nor entirely of this world out here, but is rather a kind of apocalyptic ferryman conducting us through a distorting curtain of damaged VHS color bars and across the plasma screen between worlds: the cinematic fiction of *Twin Peaks,* and the simulated real event that will be positioned at the crux of that fiction—*the atomic bomb*, detonating here at the fizzing confluence of a mythic real. Reznor's sonic incantation[26] then transports us across multiple dimensions: not only aesthetic *time*—a bridge spanning twenty-five years of pop culture—but also the time-warping membrane of our own aesthetic *perception*, from televisual media as a once-distinct category of experience to a world now so fully infused with digital imagery—*as experience*—that there is no distance at all. An apocalypse of media, in which the mirage is become the desert—from the on-demand firehose of real and unreal world images streaming into our very own hands, to the kitsch LED constellations of swarming drone light shows, to the astonishing state-of-the-art gluttony of the Las Vegas Sphere,[27] its own kind of holographic bomb as cinematic object, exploding over and over and over again upon the American Desert. "Our dreams were never the same after that," writes David Samuels of the first atomic bomb and the Sphere, "just as they will never be the same after being reshaped by a quarter of a billion pixels powered by AI. Faced with the release of a certain amount of energy, the human mind just melts."[28] The Sphere is everywhere;[29] and that daily melding is an encounter observed by Jean Baudrillard as a kind of *memorial simultaneity*, in which the *real* and the *world* are engineered in the *real time* of their own immediate annihilation—a silent, violent erasure, in which the real world in real time was never there at all, but has vaporized into the technological performance of its uncanny approximation. A *not-taking place*—as the technology of the real world in real time—so that other things not taking place, other forms of power, may actually take place in that conspiracy of narrative. Here Trent Reznor ferries us from the fiction of *Twin Peaks* into the coming detonation of a mythic fictional real. And when he has finished with his fiery crossing, he will have led us into the very reactor core of that alchemical engine room— *the neurology of show business* combusting souls as the black magic of matter, a combustion as digital cold fusion, acidly grieving the memory of this incinerated present.

She's gone
She's gone
She's gone

Minute 15

Camera sweeps across the audience. The rural Roadhouse is bigger than we remember it, bigger on the inside than is possible on its Roadhouse outside, and serving a larger public now—perhaps a regional population—with a tinge of the cavernous brewpub franchise. The globalized local of a placeless mass, sprawling like sprawl—as the architecture of *real estate,* sublimating the once Americana-rural of *Twin Peaks* into corporate hyper-suburban. There are no locals anymore. But it's a packed house, and the crowd dances on the darkened floor, engrossed and enraptured. They are there. Here. Wherever that is, in between all places.

As with every Roadhouse musical set piece, arriving at the end of each episode of *The Return,* the performance has a specific ceremonial function: to exorcise sadness from the fabric of the hour—that sadness that is the loss of the world; a necessary economy in the *Twin Peaks* nervous system, for that Lynchian sorrow is inexhaustible and must be conducted. Its source is life. Or a kind of *saudade,* as the Portuguese say—a sustained and circular mourning for something lost that can never be recovered and therefore can never be abated. To let it go would be to erase it from the memory of the world. So a sadness is lived with and nurtured as a vigil for the peril of impermanence: a longing for the loss of the world, even as it goes on. But this Roadhouse performance is tooled differently, arriving mid-episode, at the interior of the action, for it incants a coming laceration in the fabric of the world that threatens to immolate even that fount of sadness as its very life source. The voicing now is not one of sorrow, but of rage. Rage before the cauterized witness. Rage before the strobing, searing spotlight.

Minute 16

The singer howls into a demonic washboard bawl reminiscent of Killer Bob's maniacal laugh—more scoff than song—a laugh that entered Dale Cooper too when Bob finally overtook and possessed him. Reznor's derisive, Dada confrontation with the audience against a Brechtian wall of noise invokes the 1,000-yard stare of Lydia Lunch or the Cold War nerve-bursted trauma shock of Joy Division and their scathing *The Sound of Music*. His black leather-clad serial killer persona is simulative of Bad Cooper himself, as though Trent Reznor were now the double of Cooper's own fraudulent double, an imposter on *this* side of the fiction as the sinister replication attempts its predatory migration through the screen into *our* theatrical real, as a literal *double agent* on both sides of the TV.

And so we abruptly cut from the Roadhouse back to Cooper's malevolent double, his Apollonian counter-opposite, a primal Dionysian consumption glitching as the digital lobotomy that is Bad Cooper. Amid the concentric remains of the Nine Inch Nails clamoring across some reverb plate in the migraine night, Mr. C is right where we left him—lying on the South Dakota ground like a rigor mortic snow angel beneath a moonlit prairie tree. With a cavernous whoosh swelling in reverse and then clipping into the evening gentle with crickets, Mr. C suddenly sits up straight and opens his eyes, black pupils seeing into the void before him, or the void of memory inside. Bad Cooper awakening from a nightmare—or into one. He remembers.

Hard cut to black, and all sound with it.

Minute 17

Slow fade-in onto a landscape lying tenebrous beyond a foreground of high blackened ridgeline. A whorled and salt terrain more graphite and silver than black and white. High angle on a vast desert basin, dimly lit by the first glow of faintest rising daylight. It was partly cloudy in those predawn hours. A window in the rain. Thunderstorms had passed. To read of its weather report is to scan the log of an execution.

A flowing wash of soft white noise, riffling with flutter outside the fuselage window, or the convex-domed lens of a drone; a light wind scouring the meshed cage of a microphone at altitude, or the intractable hiss inside a vacuum between digital files—the arid soundscape of a landscape so sudden and epic that but for its textural, painterly formality, the photorealistic geography of the image is so utterly non-Lynchian that it immediately collapses into the uncanny well of the Lynchian vernacular, as with our own eyes we attempt to adapt to its scope and depth of field, straining to see the image at all. There is no contrivance to realism with Lynch, or the artifice of *believability,* neither of which are to be confused with the ambiguity of artistry as *experiential fact.* And the artistry of experiential fact that we now behold as landscape is a photorealism as real as geography can be.

A title-over appears, patiently, line-by-line atop the vast desert landscape, in all-caps and italicized newsprint hue, as though we are watching a newsreel, exquisitely restored:

JULY 16, 1945
WHITE SANDS, NEW MEXICO
5:29 AM (MWT)

The sudden recognition is hair-raising. To know this date, the infamy of the date—a memorial date, an inception date—screened here in the style of a *date painting* by artist On Kawara, or the truism signage of Jenny Holzer. JULY 16, 1945. As though I am standing before that Ohio billboard right here in the room: HELL IS REAL. And the turbid landscape itself now recalls the work of Trevor Paglen, whose long-range photographic images provided abstract, telescopic views onto covert US black site locations, unofficial locations somewhere out there in the miasma, but officially not there at all.[30] A countdown ensues, initiated in the remote tonal frequency of a NASA transmission—the dramaturgy of imminence as engineered fate: *Ten. Nine. Eight. Seven. Six . . .*

Camera pulls in, incrementally, toward the center of the geographic frame, at a high 45° angle, very high, and very slow—movement nearly undetectable.

Five. Four. Three.

Two.

One.

So many trees there have been along this road to Genesis. Douglas firs. The assembly line of timbers processed by the Packard Sawmill. The Arthurian circle of sycamores, and the eventual sycamore sapling that is *the evolution of the arm*, crackling with electricity. A telepathic log cradled like an infant, rescued from a forest that has burned. The moonlit gnarl of branches rising over Bad Cooper's body. The trees still out there whispering beyond the perimeter, a breeze blowing gently through them. And now *Los Alamos. The Cottonwoods.* Now the fire in the tree. The fire in the tree that is burning down heaven—

TRINITY

Camera zoom accelerates just before detonation, triggering an autonomic response in dramatic anticipation: an acceleration in my own heart rate. A rapid *beep* of ignition immediately following the terminus of the countdown—a brilliant detail in sound design signaling the pencil-pointed end of a temporal cone amplifying all of the radiant future, with no space for second thoughts, the red-button blip of no return. Then a blinding flash of white phosphorus light as if by some atmospheric flashbulb. Total whiteout accompanied by the abrupt and screeching fugue of composer Krzysztof Penderecki's *Threnody for the Victims of Hiroshima*.

As the overexposure fades, the camera continues pulling-in on the panoramic frame. A vast pool of light spreads out across the valley floor. We see a row of ten vertical smoke trails scrawling thinly upward for what must be over 1,000 feet, just right of center screen.[31] The Oscar and Mockingbird Mountains ringing the Tularosa Basin of south-central New

Mexico are pristinely illuminated in the finest detail. We may notice that we are above the scattered clouds now, shadows of their wisps passing across the ground at the crystalline resolution of a stereoscopic View-Master. We see—with the radical clarity of a sudden laser surgery. And for a moment we are granted a disembodied point of view of the first and final landscape. For a moment we are that View-Master. We are Caspar David Friedrich's *Wanderer* gazing remotely from an impossible vista into a flawless silver gelatin print, a museum-condition Ansel Adams of the El Jornada Muerto Desert, the *Dead Man's Journey.*

Minute 18

A radiant disc of shockwave plows the desert crust, excavating the terrain at hyper-geologic speed into a scrim of textured spume. At its epicenter is a mushroom cloud—a *tiny* mushroom cloud rising from an orifice of billowing jewel case pillows, the exhaust and backwash generated by the combustion of ten thousand suns on earth. The Devils Tower. A sonic Monument Valley screaming as potash and bones. The bones of bison. The bones of code. The carcasses of the future, piled and strewn

FIGURE 3 Twin Peaks: The Return © *Showtime 2017.*

as discarded strands of DNA. The scraps of every black word stolen and forged by the false sentience of the machine. The splitting of the atom, the splitting of all things at the core of being. The splitting of the bicameral garden by the tongue of the serpent into Hieronymus Bosch's memes, for each and every recombinant thing sanctioned and imagined and feral and rogue. The gorgon of that garden gazing our own image into stone, the sands of the hourglass shattered and scattered and melted into liquid crystal mirror. The black box opened by the light that burns through it. The hiss of its cooling into vacuum-sealed space. The cosmos is screaming. She is the mother of phons. Penderecki's *Threnody* at full blast radius now. Fifty-two stringed instruments, screeching like barbed wire. And the taut mahogany of hollow-bodied percussion, the Polynesian timbre of a syncopated conga line breaking toward this incinerating desert atoll, a sonic procession of late modernist assembly-line *tikis,* the chiseled supper club chins and brows of a bygone era now calcified into Easter Island stone reclining in Adirondack chairs beneath the nuclear shadow of cocktail umbrellas and *better living through chemistry.*

As we zoom in closer and closer to the ascending mushroom, we are afforded a spectacular feast of visual detail, a pornography of video sculpture unfolding in generative fractal detail: the lush, cottony surfaces of water vapor and debris cloud; the engorged and bent shaft of the stem transferring energy upward into the smoldering, ashen fireball; the dazzling interplay of light and shadow pulsating like heat lightning at the interior of the cumulonimbus firestorm—all in the rapturous resolution of an archival, black-and-white *believability,* the captivating palette of an optics shimmering between history and fiction. Unlike most phenomena in the Lynch/*Twin Peaks* universe, there is no question about what we're seeing here: the world-historic Trinity Test, conducted by the physicists, mathematicians, engineers, and United States military personnel engaged in the infamous Manhattan Project. But it's the *scale,* and the astonishing acuity of the event—at once vast and in miniature—that constitutes its cinematic potency, a radically disorienting simultaneity of scales at the most intimate of cosmic distances: the insidious, impossible clarity of drone omniscience at the altitude of Google, the sweeping scope of Landsat, but scaled to the seat-back screen of an airplane entertainment system in the *cinemascope* landscape orientation of an iPhone[32] at the scale of cataclysmic intimacy—at the scale of cosmic fear. And not only scale—but form and genre too. *What kind of media is this Trinity?* Found footage, archival documentation, educational video, documentary reenactment, stop-motion animation, AI-generation, or nuclear holocaust at the playground-proof frame-rate of Pixar? Science fiction, horror, video art, fetish film, or bomb porn. It is all of these things and a genre-defying singularity greater than its compound categories—a total work, in two minutes flat, at the annihilating intersection of all categories—gorgeous, jaw-dropping, terrifying, and sublime; a visual sequence that is as striking for its astonishing acuity and resolution as it is for its surprising irruption into the Lynchian universe, a contradictory injection of precise photographic realism into what may be his most abstract cinematic work. Trinity at the heart of *Twin Peaks*.

^o^

There would be a surging reconsideration of *the bomb* marked by Lynch's Part 8, in the years immediately surrounding *The Return*. Or perhaps a first-time, meaningful assessment of what lay at the black heart of the cultural economy, *a visitation*, on the order of an apocalyptic tourism into the mythic origins of what that culture had become, as the volume, density, and intensity of networked global intimacies metastasized into their own uncanny, reactionary, and combustible tinderbox of Virilio's cosmic fear—a bargain with the algorithmic gods mediated by increasingly leviathan and juggernaut corporate entities. Even Disney's 2016 *Rogue One: A Star Wars Story,* a prequel and the most adult entry in the franchise, introduced a direct association with the real-world technology of apocalyptic weaponry in order to see its *protagonists* climactically immolated by the searing, mushroom cloud-like shockwave from a strike by the "planet killing" Death Star as a direct setup to the 1977 origin of *Star Wars. The bomb* as an imminent set piece is everywhere in the warping timeline and cinematic fabric of the culture, as both sci-fi and dramatic realism simultaneously, mirroring its real-world intensification, and in the case of *Rogue One,* even as a coveted Christmas release just months before *Twin Peaks: The Return.*

If Stanley Kubrick's 1964 *Dr. Strangelove or: How I Learned to Stop Worrying and Love the Bomb* wrangled satire as the only viable means of getting intimate with the bomb, and *The Day After*[33] subsequently deployed terrifying *Hallmark realism* to millions of Sunday evening viewers, we circle closer and closer now to a dramaturgy of that apocalyptic fictional real, a fictional real foreshadowed by the astonishing production design of HBO's 2019 *Chernobyl,* an aesthetic recapitulation of the entire project and catastrophe of Western Civilization, in which the fiction of that *production design is the historical present.* In its rigorous, critically acclaimed artistry, the reactor core of *Chernobyl* is repurposed as a mythic crucible for the transcribing of its own historic mythos into *content,* an apocalyptic tourism as the means by which its players and participants spectate in that apocalyptic myth as a grand reflecting device—apocalypse as the means by which it is possible to have a perspective on the hyperobject of ourselves that is too big to see. *The royal view.* A cumulative upgrade in the breadth and resolution of that impossible, symbolic view that was accessed by the prehistoric mound builders in their execution of the Ohio Serpent Mound, a form, in its finished state, which they could not see—now as that total archive of all possible images, prehistoric and as yet unrealized, at our fingertips.

As our own way of seeing undergoes radical transformation, the corresponding sea change in the total culture reassesses and reappropriates its core mythic constellation as central to the total transformation: that invisible center, which is everywhere, as its combustion chamber, its globally distributed perforation as an ontological respiration. *The world* is increasing in density and intensity, surging in the simultaneous countercurrents of neurological *intimacy* and *isolation*, and the uncanny performance of its *familiarity as Other*, which may be described visually as a radical increase in *resolution* corresponding precisely to a degradation in *fidelity*. The higher the resolution of its self-image, the lower its fidelity to itself. The overrepresentation of the world results in a perception of the world itself as an uncanny valley. The uncanny valley of the world. The world is annihilated and instantly reborn as imposter—at the speed of fiberoptic. Alien Nation.[34] In which it is easier to imagine the end of the world than it is to imagine the world.[35] *Apocalypse* as a mode of seeing, reappropriated and replicated as the spectacular, archival content of itself—as streaming story, as endless series, meme, and sequel to itself. In this, and in the incessant procession of Hollywood remakes as the capital real estate of content—an entire cultural economy of remakes and sequels, encompassing even the build-up to the 2024 presidential election as spectacularly glitching rerun—it seems that David Lynch has been prescient in his peculiar obsession with the pervasiveness and malevolence of the double, the doppelgänger. And now the Lynchian reality-doppelgänger of *Apocalypse*.

In what is sure to be a twenty-first-century revisitation of *The Day After* at runaway global scale, *Blade Runner* and *Dune* franchise maestro Denis Villeneuve will produce Annie Jacobsen's *Nuclear War: A Scenario*, a nonfiction account of the hypothetical chain of events and outcome of a full-scale international nuclear war—in which, due to the algorithms and automations of response, there are ultimately no culprits but the stockpile of weapons and weapon systems themselves, a profound malevolence found in a kind of proto-AI, or the inhuman network of ourselves, generated by us: *a totalitarian infrastructure of us*. A conspiratorial iteration of ourselves over which we have no control but are unwittingly, collectively responsible—a terrifying narrative agency that is simultaneously hegemonic, invisible, and automated. A conspiracy of the real.

In the inciting incident of Cormac McCarthy's final, twin novels *The Passenger* and *Stella Maris* (2022), a passenger plane is mysteriously downed and lost at sea. When the sunken fuselage is eventually found and recovered, an unidentified passenger and the black box flight recorder have vanished. The data keys to the conspiracy itself—as plot points—are absent. We never learn the identity of the missing passenger or the contents of the black box, the meaning of their disappearance, or their meaning at all. Instead, we are left in an elliptical orbit about that void: the conspiracy of a gaping hole in the plot and a conspiracy of no plot at all—a conspiracy of the missing conspiracy itself. The conspiracy is the ruptured artifice of narrative as a function of language, cored of its human fungibility: that things must mean something. In *The Return*, Lynch's black box—his flight recorder—is transparent and occupying the center of the room as a sculptural seeing machine, a four-dimensional reflecting device in which the encrypted archival container has been turned inside out and is emptying itself into the world as the *contents* of the world. An emptying emptiness, in which the watchers are watching the watchers watching, waiting for something to happen. When what is happening is that very watching, again and again and again, in the obfuscating obliteration between the world and its symbolic representation. In this endlessly glitching present of 2017's *The Return* (and beyond—), we are the watchers watching. *The plot is the conspiracy*, unrelenting, ever-unresolved; and it is the viewers who are ultimately annihilated by the face-mauling wrath of *the experiment*: the viewers themselves as sacrificial voyeurs to that conspiracy, in which Trinity is the device, radiating in all temporal directions, inward and outward from *Twin Peaks*.

The protagonists of McCarthy's *Stella Maris* and *The Passenger* are their own kind of twin device, particles split and colliding about that centrifugal narrative void. Bobby and Alicia Western are incestuously intimate siblings and children of the Manhattan Project, their father a physicist of such competence that he worked alongside J. Robert Oppenheimer himself, director of the Los Alamos Laboratory and "father of the atomic bomb." Through this fated pair, McCarthy peers inside the human legacy of Trinity adrift, the children of its engineers reckoning with the psychological fallout of its most remote mathematical frontiers and a society that trades in the conspiracy of that probability as a bone-crushing vacuum at the *unreal* center of its fraudulent assertions: its fraudulent reassurances of humanity, refuge, and mercy. With his final works, McCarthy placed a capstone on his position as literary master of the phantasmagoric pathos and predatory carnage of the mythic American landscape. Following upon the final lyric pages of *The Crossing*, and the gorgeous minimalism and searing austerity of *The Road*, *The Passenger* contains what might be the most devastating prose ever put to paper on the subject of the bomb at Trinity, Hiroshima, and Nagasaki.[36]

"War was always here. Even before man was, war waited for him. The ultimate trade awaiting its ultimate practitioner,"[37] McCarthy writes in *Blood Meridian*. Spoken by the fictional Judge Holden, this infamous declaration of the ultimate trade awaiting its ultimate practitioner is articulated as a *literary truth*, corroborated by the visceral, cinematic severity, primal essentialism, and indeed historical fiction of the book itself— as *proof*. That literary sleight-of-hand, or device, though, is revealed by replacing the word "war" with "music" or "language" or "cinema" or "the internet" or nearly any other universal human endeavor. *Music was always here. Even before man was, music waited for him. . . .* Yet here—at the Trinity *Test*—that "truth" of war is contingently proven in the harnessing of all human and earthly resources—the cumulative technology of the entirety of civilization marshaled toward the engineering of this single and final weapon of war, a singularity of human coordination, ingenuity, and reason; and a singularity containing its existential antithesis, its ontological double: psychopathic disintegration, absurd stupidity, and savagery. And Lynch *shows it to us* as the axiomatic *icon* that it is—the juxtaposition of extreme duality as Lynchian revelation.

McCarthy and Lynch, two giants of postwar American art, centering the metaphysical texture of the atomic bomb at the apotheoses of their landmark careers—perhaps anticipating a reckoning yet coming.[38] An existential threat of unprecedented horror is upon us now again—in 2025—rearing its monstrous invisible head in the full force of broad daylight news from an underground nest of silos that never went away, but returns in the cycles of cognitive dissonance and denial of itself as *unbelievably* real. A living-with, as in the stained-glass conservatory of some horrendous spectral *saudade*, the cicadas that shed their husks as blast-fired skeletal phantoms, everywhere clinging to trees.

In 2023, Christopher Nolan tackled the narrative breadth of the Manhattan Project directly, taking us inside a sweeping fictional historicization and dramatized political bureaucracy of the Trinity Test with his auteur-studio tentpole production *Oppenheimer*, an Oscar-sweeping *event* curated at the scale of the entire cultural economy. *Oppenheimer*, of course, came with its own doppelgänger, the much-hystericized *Barbie*, its own product-genre of post-Trinity culturally dysmorphic mutation. Together, *Oppenheimer* and *Barbie* were a complimentary rehabilitation of the *apocalyptic franchise*: in which the cultural economy rebrands the *branding* of itself as an apocalyptic regeneration—the perpetual transfiguration of itself into content as a cancerous fractal of infinite growth. Sentient space as real estate. The trauma-cinema of prestige devastation and controlled hysteria as collective illumination. *Oppenheimer* made exceptional use of dramatic realism as a hyper-subjectivity, a subjectivity at its cinematic and physiological extreme reduced to the frame rate of ventilation: Cillian Murphy's Robert Oppenheimer himself breathing in the hyperbaric chamber of his own moment-by-moment confrontation with cosmic fear as cosmic truth—the moment of truth of the Trinity Test— the wavelengths of his own respiration an atomic clock dividing frames of audience experience into units of sublime terror, separating failure of the Test from the total ignition of the planetary atmosphere. It's a stunning sequence of *breathtaking*, rendering Nolan's film effective, at least, as hysterical historicization.

But at minute 18 of Part 8, Lynch steps into that vacuum of breathlessness, taking us beyond and inside the engineered history-as-entertainment where all of the oxygen has been sucked right out of the room. Lynch rescues Trinity from its perpetual appropriation as *content* in the replicant real—the real estate of the sacrificial cultural economy of perpetually glitching apocalypse—and installs it as a holographic memorial monument, illuminating a total landscape of shared temporality. Here, as with *The Day After,* in its disorientation of scale, genre, and ontological category, Lynch generates *this* bomb—*his* Trinity—as a circuit of meaning described by Werner Herzog in his *Minnesota Declaration* as an *ecstatic truth,* a cinematic encounter suspended not between fiction and fact, but between fiction and truth. An artistic truth defying and transcending both fact and fiction—as each other; a poetic truth sufficiently probed neither by a so-called cinéma vérité of pure, non-interventionist documentation nor by spectacular fictions that aspire to high-concept realism or high-concept fantasy—but a truth ecstatic, one that can only be accessed by an intention toward acknowledging a deeper fluidity and uncanny mediation between states of experience.[39]

In the cosmic space of Lynch's two-minute Trinity sequence, we've crossed over the radically permeable membrane—or *medium*—between cinematic fiction as entertainment, and entertainment as social fabric; from an alternate fictional universe into a media of the historically real.[40] To encounter Lynch's Trinity-site at the temporal coordinate of its ecstatic truth is to embark on a cinematic pilgrimage. Of all the real and unreal moving images[41] produced in this century thus far—and the towering tsunami of all yet to come—Lynch's Trinity challenges the tensile strength of the fourth wall as the mediating membrane of *believability* more than any I've encountered. A sequence impossible, yet true. His state-of-the-art simulation is not accomplice or antagonist to the action, neither background to the plot nor set piece to be occupied and reckoned with by characters. Lynch's Trinity *is* the character, and it is the action—a *sculptural event* as the sentient mirror of the art-object at the resolution of Hollywood. Trinity is us seeing ourselves as witness to it. It is reality itself that is at stake here, not the veracity of its representation; a kind of Voight-Kampff Test[42] gauging not the categorical authenticity of the uncanny other, but the tuning of my own human nervous system embedded in the replicant real. Lynch's Trinity stands at the frontier of the *fifth wall*, that border crossing into a total encounter with total fiction—*experience itself as content*. Lynch's Trinity *is* Trinity, strobing as a real McCoy in the uncanny valley of my own networked and morphing contemporary experience.

By positioning the historical Trinity as central to the cycle of a personal and deeply fictional pantheon, Lynch—in the transference and transfusion of art-making—upholds the world's first nuclear test explosion as the epicenter of a nationally and globally shared symbolic real. Trinity is pinned to the overlapping maps of *Twin Peaks* and America as the triangulation of a mythic coordinate, the temporal orientation point of a concentrically radiating benchmark. If *Twin Peaks* was a speculative vivisection of the subterranean pathos of America, festering in broad daylight, Trinity is both the source of that pathos *and* the source of its illumination, blasting through the overlapping maps of the fictional and the consequential, and rendering them as transparencies—a work of holographic *land art* as a national monument. Lynch's Trinity is Mt. Rushmore *and* Lascaux, before us, right now, on the cave wall of the immediate holographic present, and we are witness to it—from the scale of its *cinematic reality*—as a monument in the mythic real, a holographic cairn standing at the blacklight crossroads of the cosmos and the Anthropocene. In the shadow cast by that twentieth-century Golgotha, in the blind spot of the contemporary, Lynch has switched on the nightlight.

^o^

The artist William Kentridge draws a connection between the *agency* of seeing images and a violence inherent in the power of fixing their interpretation and adjudication. In his lecture series *Six Drawing Lessons*,[43] Kentridge critiques Plato's foundational cave allegory from an uncommon angle: arguing the functional merit of the visual *illusion*, or the necessity of the cave itself, in opposition to an accepted teleological liberation toward "the truth." In Plato's narrative hierarchy, the illusory or cinematic shadow-theatre of fraudulent images projected upon the wall of the cave progresses logically toward the ultimate vesting of power in an authoritative entity as the sole arbiter of illumination, or knowledge of the cave's true nature—the nature of representation—on behalf of the spectating citizenry. The chaining to illusion, or the manufactured opiate of misdirection projected within the cave, and the violence inherent and perhaps inevitable in its mediation is a question of agency. As Kentridge puts it:

> For Plato's philosopher who journeys out of the cave there is moral and political right through a correct understanding of the relationship of that which is seen, an internal process, to the world outside, external to us. On the basis of this understanding, the philosopher gains the right and obligation to be king. In other words, the knowledge bestows the right to power, which is always a right to violence.[44]

A violence is administered both in keeping spectators enslaved to a perception of untruths *and* in freeing them from that false perception toward some other more transcendent truth. Violence then, as the ultimate instrument of power, is delivered in both directions, up and down the hierarchy of seeing: in the initial holding of *captives of perception* to the cave's interior screen and in their obligatory teleological deliverance from it; and then in turn as "the control of violence exercises a monopoly on accepted knowledge,"[45] or the *security* necessary in maintaining a monopoly on prescribed illumination. Thus the generation of a subsequent cave is necessitated for the restricted dissemination of accepted knowledge. The allegory of the cave then implies the generation of more and more caves as means of liberation from the cave, in an endless chain of multiple caves projected upon caves within caves, with no original or end in sight. Itself a kind of compound optical illusion, or kaleidoscopic mineral structure comprised of only projector, only cave. A kind of *lifelike* optical crypto-lichen growing upon the wall of itself as an IMAX psyop.

But to see the cave at all, the images upon its wall, the engineering of a projector, and the possibility of deliverance up the ladder of illumination—as a floral VanderMeerian structure—is to presuppose the possibility for an *agency of seeing* amid rigorous uncertainty, or the artfulness of ambiguity as a heterogeneity of perception. An agency of seeing that allows for the possibility of *illusion as illumination* in the field of images and in the project of knowledge-making as a non-passive encounter—a seeing that *requires* illusion as proof of its agency!—the agency that Lynch, and all challenging filmmakers, require of us. Then the violence of illumination may also be encountered and seen for what it is, a radical and vertiginous deepening of the perception of our own experience itself as being utterly liquid between belief and disbelief:

That we require the cave in order to also roam freely from it—as a circuit of illusion and illumination, an artistry of disbelief in belief, and belief in disbelief. To enter and exit at will, amid the flood of the synaptic, cinematic world. Then, Kentridge ventures, "we the audience [become] the performers, our act that of believing and disbelieving in the same moment . . . The pleasure in the moment of us believing and disbelieving is a jolt of self-assertion. This split, believer and disbeliever, becomes a crack in Plato's edifice."[46] This fission is an act of agency, "allowing us to be neither the prisoners in the cave, unable to comprehend what we see, nor the all-seeing philosopher returning with all his certainty. But allowing us to inhabit the terrain in between, the space between what we see on the wall and what we conjure up in our retinas."[47]

It is precisely this terrain of in-between space and rigorous ambiguity in the field of images that Lynch conjures as *sublime orientation* inside the cinematic cave of his Trinity

Test: a documentary simulation-as-representation of the impossibly unreal real. By isolating his nuclear set piece from the established apocalyptic genre, and re-contextualizing it as an unflinching *Lynchian real*, Lynch frees Trinity from patronizing and pedagogic modes of entertainment, moral, and archival frameworks alike, and positions the historic event as a living artifact, a *(non)fiction* animating the twin ethos and pathos of the culture as a combusting simultaneity. Trinity as an autonomous and *really existing* world meme, as a poetic antidote to the violence of forced illumination by that power which has generated it. Sublime deliverance as sublime orientation to the ecstatic truth that Trinity resides both interior and exterior to our apparatus of seeing, as archetypal iconography. *I am what I see*: a Trinity that has demanded agency of its viewer and subsequently bestows it.[48]

How long I had been waiting for Trinity. How long had I been waiting for it to reverse engineer out of *Super America*. To be put back. For thirty-four years—from *The Day After* to *The Return*—a thermonuclear hologram firing the cathode-ray snow globe in my hands. A great dark magnet humming at the center of the cinematic country, throbbing with neuralgia at the core of a culture excruciating and numbed by total mirage. Haunting from the inside out, a phantom rear projection burning and looping across the lenses of my visual cortex. A transcendent Thanatos in the society that has oriented itself by ecstatic apocalypse above all else, by its very fabric.[49] And then suddenly it was there.[50] Burning through celluloid, blooming in the desert of crystalline nucleation and pristine digital freeze—as a national monument. The hallucinatory cairn of Trinity soldered by Lynch to the center of that spectral plain as a lightning rod for the electric crimes of civilization: atonement by the tremor-bearing lodestone of art—the *uselessness* of art but for that alchemical confession. Orienting me—not by what things mean, but to its *composition*. The spell of its canting stone set upon a land of superstition.

Lynch has conducted us, via cinematic seance, over the threshold of a compromised American dream and out onto the proving ground of that mythic corruption. By the *medium* of Trent Reznor's Nine Inch Nails, in summoning the parasitized memory of Cooper's doppelgänger as a reanimated Bad Cooper, we are *transponded* to the coordinates of that haunted space wherein all that follows and all that remains is the mirage of an artifice shone through by that terrible light. The terrible truth of the falsity of all things seeking repair in the half-light, the blacklight of a dead star that will not be extinguished and whose location is marked by the radiating, holographic now: the black site of America. The entomological patterns and angelic hallucinations that are the effervescent nightmare of a society's metabolism; its accursed artifact, a state of such extreme combustion and catastrophe that it collapses into symbolic space; and simultaneously the reverse: a state of such extreme symbolic combustion that it collapses back into the catastrophe of all of space, cosmic space. Cosmic symbolism and cosmic space combusting back and forth, as the circuit of each other, powering a cinema that defies both representation *and* the real, at the extreme perimeter of that circuit, venturing where it is not humanely possible to venture. So Lynch does just that. He guides us inside a perceptual, neuropathic encounter with Trinity itself, inside the very tactile fabric of the Trinity Test as a cinematic object, a kind of seeing machine, as the *art* of seeing where no one has ever seen before—the raging, interior core of Trinity as the atomic landscape of ourselves, haunting us from the inside out.

Minute 19

Camera *enters* the mushroom cloud, attaining a point of view where none is possible, where there is no camera, where there is no point of view at all. And then—just as radically—there is: in the breaching of the blood-blast barrier, a transfusion of aesthetic medium occurs once more as the *literal* possibilities of CGI collapse into the *optical* artistry of analog technique.

Squibs of black plasma bursting into clouds of squid ink on filmed glass slides. A sunrise of blood orange and mango lens flare searing through the eyelids of a test blast witness. A glissando of fulminating honey bees descending from the bulbous and blistering hive. The delirious perturbations of photons hatching like flies, half-moon and eclipsing against the black firmament of a nuclear emulsion plate flurrying with readings off the chart. An orchestral chord in air-raid baritone[51] sounding the *cut-up* to a Sartrean maelstrom of quivering cilia, hairs of spermatozoa, or sprouting fungi spasmodic for a chance at life against the gauze.

Minute 20

Then a high-contrast blizzard racing within a light source just out of frame, the crushing loneliness of a remote Dakota gas field; or a pestilence of discarded data debris swarming silently in the ventilation shaft at the center of all data farms; insurance-protocol security-cam logging the Kafkan queasiness at a unitary multitude of *thingnesses*, then accelerating into an electrical storm of magnetic filaments *sketching* and convulsing into epileptic and angry murmurations—a hypnotic and patternless flickering that if paused[52] would freeze on a poltergeist of chalk marks on blackboard, each frame a unique and individual artwork in a series of furious Cy Twombly agitations. The interior of Trinity as art school, or the optic nerve of cinematography itself—the physically cosmic abstractions of Stan Brakhage; Kubrick's visionary *2001 Stargate Sequence*; Malick's transcendental *Tree of Life*;[53] the decaying emulsified nitrate film sequences of Bill Morrison; or the tunnel of 16mm psychedelic terror through which Gene Wilder ferries his adolescent brood of vices in the 1971 *Willie Wonka and the Chocolate Factory*—and here Lynch fearlessly upholds a dramaturgy that the experience of his work is not representational, is not symbolic, is not *about,* but tactilely *is,* symbolic of itself as aesthetic incantation, as subcutaneous pageantry, as phantom musicality, summoning the *Sesame Street*[54] semaphore of Malevich and Kandinsky; the geologic solar panels of Rothko; the symphonic psycho-geographies of Jorge Queiroz, and of course the figurative fugue-states of Francis Bacon. The secret never revealed—but now *illuminated by the unity of Trinity*—is that the crux of the Lynchian uncanny is that its interpretation (or decoding) is ever beyond the horizon of the event itself. With no distance between itself and its meaning, the Lynchian cinematic event is hermetically sealed as an ontological dyad: simultaneously what it is and what it is not, with no daylight in between but the sublime angst of that irresolvable contradiction in radiant decay.

Fire and smoke enveloping everything, devouring perception. Then shifting to a palette of super-saturated technicolor hemorrhaging softly into lethal irises, floral and kaleidoscopic, penetrating a surface slush of cellulite. Fireworks of photopigment exploding through the colonoscopic film gate at multiple rotating rupture points, an esophagus choking on the rhizoidal blooming of volcanic firelight, purging in ribbed spasms of sonar ejaculation, and then flaring into a total herniating inflammation.

Minute 21

Penderecki's ongoing score briefly falls apart, breaking down and then reassembling into a yowling harpy. Penderecki himself passed away in proximity to *The Return*—just a few years later, during Covid—so I listened to his avant-garde masterpiece again, against the world, carving out sonic space against polytempic apocalyptic speeds: the slow-motion still-life unfolding outside our apartment window as we meanwhile fast-forwarded into the controlled madness of interior Berlin winter lockdown with a five-year-old child; this temporal smearing occurring amid a migration into the interior-exterior light speed of totally online life. Penderecki's *Threnody*[55] was a fitting and devastating score to that daily well of loss, a total loss as the suspension of the timecode of the world, and the cacophony of its minute-by-minute observation—the timecode of a cinematic real[56] combusting pixel by pixel into silent scream.

Now Lynch returns Penderecki's *Threnody to the Victims of Hiroshima* to the context of its 1961 memorial purpose, *observing the instance* of those victims by dropping his camera into the very core of that incineration, and amplifying the impossible interior of that combustion as *fire, and more fire, and more fire.* Overwhelming, overtaking, all-consuming fire, the likes of which we've not seen before from Nolan nor Herzog nor *National Geographic* alike. A gorgeous, terrible, mesmerizing combustion of fire and fire and more fire. Lynch's favorite element and favored texture. If fish are the shape of water, the liquid behavior of ideas, then fire is the shape of cinema, the illuminating, thermodynamic entropy of that idea, here at the source of it, at the molten core of Trinity as a cinematic crucible. Fire and smoke as a total oceanic environment, as living aesthetic surface in every conceivably hue of visible heat-index—electric violets and fuchsias, blinding magentas, scarlet, and ruby reds scorching into charred and cauterized gunpowder, the blackest of blacks with no volume or mass or forgiveness at all, just cinema as burning light and consequences, until every last quantum of color has been seared from the screen and we are blown across by a correspondent's final salvaged frames of black-and-white firestorm roiling into blackout.

Minute 22

Yet we are not relieved, neither of the *Threnody* nor of its consequences. The symphonic, experimental fugue enters its third act. A meningitis in the provinces—and what is certainly among Lynch's crowning theatrical set pieces.[57]

Single setup. Locked camera position. Full frame. This is important. We're not engineering a naturalism here—a believability—but a *theatrical* mise en scéne in which the production design is the plot; the setting is the event; and the on-location practical execution and post-production visual impressionism are in total visionary alignment. In an age when visually anything is possible, Lynch yet manages to generate pictures from the far side of the valley, images that seem utterly analog, yet are so bewildering that our own perception of them is rewired by a kind of witchcraft. The impression of handcraft is endowed with magic: the *special effect* is that we have no idea how he's done what he's done. It is not sufficient to answer, "CGI," which does nothing to address the organic puzzle and elation of: *what am I seeing here and how am I seeing it?*

A FILLING STATION CONVENIENCE STORE

Black and white. Darkest night. A derelict gas station somewhere, we may presume, in the desert vicinity of the Trinity Site. A pair of antique gas pumps on the poor, dirt lot are each crowned with a single bare bulb, ornamental company globes long gone, broken, or stolen. A flashing association with Great Depression locations photographed by the great Walker Evans;[58] and *Twin Peaks'* own Big Ed's Gas Farm.[59]

The clapboard storefront door is banging arrhythmically, glitching open and closed as if by a ragged wind seizing through a stop-action ghost town. But the trees next to the station are still and muted inside Penderecki's continuing score. A weathered phone booth stands open and shrouded in shadow aside the storefront window. An exterior staircase rises up the side of the building, disappearing from view but terminating at an angle near an outdoor light just above the convenience store where there is no second floor. We are as close as we may get to the physical location of the mythic *room above a convenience store*—another disturbing and spectral antechamber to the

Black Lodge—a room that is not there at all, but for convening in the acetate revelation of the blacklight.

A rapid pulse in the key lighting as some power fluctuation surging through the whistle stop crossroads of a mini model train set. The convenience store's front door is frozen open by an *entity of smoke* spilling out into the lot in an audio washboard of digital distortion skipping like wasp paper machine gun fire. The *Threnody* swells into a swarming hive of strings as the plume of smoke bursts further and further out the door and then is sucked back up inside the shop again in a jarring sequence of stop-action frames dialing forward and backward and further forward until the interior of the convenience store is flashing and flaring with white-hot light blasting butcher's block white through the plate-glass windows, fulminating as the lethal vitrine of an experimental executioner's chamber. *Smoking*.

FIGURE 4 Twin Peaks: The Return © *Showtime 2017.*

Minute 23

Woodsmen entering abruptly from the curtain of smoke now ricocheting around the abandoned filling station. The very Woodsmen who cupped and culled the demonic, parasitic gut-sac of Killer Bob from within the guts of Mr. C. An apparitional horde of these scorched and bearded frontiersmen clearing the smoke, clearing the score, and now glitching around the lot in an agitation of schizoid digital stutter cutting in and out of a cottony vacuum of digital silence. Woodsmen milling hurriedly, pacing a worried urgency, dropping frames about the pump island. A nerve. A great unrest.

Finally, a cut-in from the master shot confirms a glimpse of canned goods stacked in pyramids on shop tables inside the convenience store. No doubt they are cans of creamed corn, or *garmonbozia*,[60] animate in the spell of electrical firelight pulsating inside the storefront windows.

Minute 24

Then the Woodsmen are gone, and the entire gas station minimart is strobing and shorting, all ashen and blindingly bright, a seizure of ungrounded current alternating back and forth from interior to exterior, sizzling in the mega-voltage of electromagnetic shock to its system. *Electrocution.* A neural blitzkrieg catalyzed by some maniacally invisible hand flipping the master switch: *Super America*[61]—not bombed-out or burned but *fried* and blazing phosphorus and singed into the photo-plate night, a great bug zapper casting its atomic light into the hyperbolic absurdity of superabundance that it would become, too much of itself to bear its own weight, a horde of *horde,* warping out of focus in the frequency-distortion of supply chain gone haywire while the wraiths of that boomtown polis scrape creosote and bitumen from the walls of the future well run dry, convulsing, quivering, quaking, shaking, and concussing into a foghorn of anaphylactic blackout.

A paranormal, pataphysical space opened up now in the tremor of that neuropathic trauma. The agony of that cauter is a rotten cavity of anguish. A space activated and weaponized by Trinity in which ALL SPACE is weaponized—*another place* nowhere here inside the cosmic fear of the world.

The atomic hollow of Jowday.

Wherein scowls the wrath of Judy.

She is there. Floating in intra-chthonic space like a larval Macy's Day parade balloon. The angle and trajectory of her leucistic form giving shape and direction to the black void itself, filling it with the proto-incarnation of *her self*, her bitter clay. The existential body, anemic and lethal, a vengeance of the skinless suffering of being itself, as if Henry's[62] own *Eraserhead* baby were denied metamorphosis and—in recapitulating the angry phylogeny of itself—grew up to become its own aggrieved and orphaned mother, an entity scorned and mutant to the chain of the real finally ruptured in the ignition of matter into pathos:[63] *the experiment.*[64] Her backward-turned thumbs,[65] the nubs of devils' horns, barren vestigial breasts, and needlepoint eyes. She retches, a marvelous foley of gurgling and rale concussing from somewhere deep inside the boiler room, and from her cloaca where a mouth might have been vomits forth a long cable of umbilical semen, a viscous rope of amniotic spermaceti, the ectoplasmic garmonbozia or *creamed corn* of the malevolent leviathan: the ambient matter of "pain and sorrow" condensed into a pustulous discharge of *symbolic substance.*[66]

Minute 25

Pulling in on the lengthening train of projectile spew, a *production* filled with the detritus of infection, or some kind of horrific insemination—small eggs of varying sizes, hard-shelled and speckled as a killdeer's clutch floating throughout the gelatinous mucus; and among them, a larger meteorite-encrusted pod, the spore of Killer Bob, absurdly adult-faced and ovoviviparous, peering wild-eyed and sadistic from inside the same spherical caul of frogspawn that the woodsman would draw from the guts of Bad Cooper (later in the timeline, but earlier in the timecode). As he passes us by, birthing from the gelatinous goop,[67] a subordinate egg in proximity also detaches, almost incidentally, and is released into space.

Entering into the petroleum product itself now, among the suspended eggs and germinal blisters of gaseous ova. Passing deeper inside the *composition* of the interior matter—

FIRE FIRE FIRE FIRE FIRE FIRE FIRE FIRE FIRE FIRE
FIRE FIRE FIRE FIRE FIRE FIRE FIRE FIRE FIRE FIRE FIRE
FIRE FIRE FIRE FIRE FIRE FIRE FIRE FIRE FIRE FIRE FIRE
FIRE FIRE FIRE FIRE FIRE FIRE FIRE FIRE FIRE FIRE FIRE
FIRE FIRE FIRE FIRE FIRE FIRE FIRE FIRE FIRE FIRE FIRE
FIRE FIRE FIRE FIRE FIRE FIRE FIRE FIRE FIRE FIRE FIRE
FIRE FIRE FIRE FIRE FIRE FIRE FIRE FIRE FIRE FIRE FIRE
FIRE FIRE FIRE FIRE FIRE FIRE FIRE FIRE FIRE FIRE FIRE

Combustion raging with such irruption as we had not yet seen, screaming from the very psychic fiber of interstitial sentience. And *producing gold*.

Minute 26

A bead of gold[68] emerges from the white-hot eye of the firestorm, a globule of gold nugget[69] turning slowly as an asteroid and traveling toward the camera, like a golden bead of mercury or a golden Anish Kapoor reflecting fire all around it, itself but the shape of that reflection, until we are so close upon it that the reflection itself becomes substance, the molten golden substance of the form—and we enter *it*. Interiorities within interiorities, enfolded within the circulation of each other. A vascular flow of the life-giving elixir. The bloodstream of it, racing with plasma: the matte latex paintballs of a flawless digital worlding—a galactic interior countless with red blood cells pounding through the cosmological siphon of this heart and its chambers: fire, gold, wind, electricity. The four cardinal elements of the *Twin Peaks* compass[70] speeding now through elemental space—

And cross-dissolving to another *landscape.*

Minute 27

A darkened purple night sea, tempestuous, foreboding, and swirling with foam and purple whitecaps sweeping beneath us. We're traveling across it now, in first person, as it were. The camera's perspective is ours—as it always is—but now it's no one else's: a great loneliness of subjectivity, as a vampire in flight from the alone to the alone. A liquid crystalline terrain, without dimension, and pulsating with the sense that it's never been encountered before. It exists only here, deeper and deeper inside the cranial chambers of these cinematic catacombs. The terra incognita of an enzymatic sea.

A remarkable feat, the elation of a singular image, rare amid the superabundance of digital imagery that comprises contemporary experience, not only for its sudden, inexplicable appearance—here, inside *Twin Peaks*—but also for its tactile contradictions as a composition: a whorling *purple* sea[71] *behaving* realistically, yet fantastically digital, elemental, chaotic, patterned, infinite, repeating; a saline viscosity of diluted *ink,* the resolution of a moving, painterly landscape. A Turner seascape as video game background, monochrome and turbulent, and no action at all. Traces of *Eraserhead* set here too in the industrial chiaroscuro of toxic spill; as the bouffant coiffure and facial hives pocking Lynch's mushroom cloud signaled an *Eraserhead* topography—generating a diptych bound in Sisyphean gravitas: the crepuscular Trinity Site and this alkaline purple sea.

A feature appears on the black horizon. Land. A rocky mountain spire rising out of the purple sea and into the black and purple night. Not sky, but interminable *night*. Perhaps the scabbard peak of some colossal underwater island; again an immensity of scale, but also in miniature, as though we are not in an exterior landscape at all, but within a great interior, inside some opaque and murky dome at the limit of an inhuman architecture. The edge of the frame is not the constraint of a selected visual field, but the end of reality itself—a medieval futurism rounded into the hollow of a *space mountain*. Video game space, beyond which the map of the perceptible world simply terminates into an abyss of code dissolving and deleting into a void of Logos.

A fizz of digital spindrift whirls into fine patterns from the purple ocean swelling and spraying about great forbidding rocks where the crag falls into the sea. A gale without temperature and bracing from no pressure system at all, a wind that one imagines never ceases, but just as suddenly might. The massif towering before us is eclipsed in total shadow but for the fine and flinty lines of its contours glinting in some starboard purple ghost light, and our ascension of it summons from the dark memory of cinema's dark and archetypal mountain forms: Leni Riefenstahl's proto-*heimat*[72] film *Das Blau Licht* (1932); Fritz Lang's looming, expressionist set pieces and allegorically crafted Tower of Babel from his ur-film *Metropolis* (1928); even the iconic Devils Tower, featured in Spielberg's *Close Encounter of the Third Kind* (1977); and above all, Disney's wicked *Night on Bald Mountain* from *Fantasia* (1940). On Riefenstahl's infamous dark mountain motif, Susan Sontag observes and demystifies: "As usual the mountain is represented as both supremely beautiful and dangerous, that majestic force which invites the ultimate affirmation of and escape from the self—into the brotherhood of courage and death."[73] Yet there we travel, upward into that annihilating mysticism.

Lynch *animates* the archetype as his own, and here we are the live-action protagonist, answering the internal call that cannot be refused. Our effortless ascension of the black rock at sea—as if by drone—is an ascension of the psyche, an ascension of souls upon the body of that psyche. The video idiom of drone flight is recovered here from the ubiquitous artifice of corporate techno-populism, or *drone advertising* as the omniscient surveillance of the real, and alchemically repurposed as an astral travel. There is no drone here at all. Our eyes are closed, seeing inside, as geography collapses into *sensing*. We are not tourists mobile about the real estate of content, but travelers venturing into the interior mountain of the world, anchored upon its colossal foundation reclining further and further into the diminishing perspective of its soaring inaccessibility until it may demure no higher, and we behold it.

Minute 28

The luminous citadel of the poesies. Brutalist[74]—yet glowing, milky, rounded, and smoothed as an architect's foam board model, but for the fine mortared seams of skim-coated cinderblock, gleaming in cold moonlight—and integrating two architectural modes of a formal, bureaucratic mysticism. A *bureau* of mysticism:

On the right, the Fibonacci nautilus of Frank Lloyd Wright's Manhattan Guggenheim, coiled beneath a great handled arch—a cosmopolitan space devoted to the decadence of aesthetic surfaces as experiential depths in and of themselves. And on the left, the sheer and colossal escarpment walls of Orthodox Athos, Meteroa, Bhutan, or Lhasa's Potala Palace, rising between two monolithic domes—remote monastic enclaves dedicated to the codices of cosmic principles, or the arcane metadata of those infinite surfaces. Integrated here—is there any difference between these two halls? At the core of each is the architectural expression of an *observatory* of paranormal phenomena, *the art-sciences,* a gnosis reverse engineering the soul's mercurial forms as occult cartography: the mapping of our own azimuth as a stellar body in the circumambulating now. *What am I? How can this possibly be?* What is the tone and timbre of that shockwave corona resulting from the intersection of these two mysteries? Readings of light emitted from the perpetual collision of twin black holes.

Droning up the sheer wall of the unscalable tower, it tilts forward to the angle of our approach as if granting optical permission for entry, and we ascend toward a lone window positioned at the highest reaches of the fortress, the tiniest rectangular opening in the concrete signaling the true enormity of the building's scale, inaccessible and unassailable as the notched vertical portal to a peregrine falcon's keep.

Minute 29

Droning in on the open window, a brute opening in the stone, until it fills the frame in full, and we enter—into a swelling of cavernous darkness. The length or duration of its passage gives some indication of the depth of the structure's fortification, and then it suddenly gives way to an unexpected and marvelously lush interior: a vintage *parlor* infusing art deco and art nouveau styles into a baroque saturation of black-and-white printed design.

Señorita Dido is seated upon a sumptuous chaise lounge before a decorative iron screen. She sways gently to the opioid rotations of a speakeasy gramophone, crackling softly beyond the end of the sofa. At the front left of the salon sits a large black bell-shaped device, perhaps fabricated of iron, copper, or tin. Two small round gauges are displayed on its hull, and two insulated electromagnetic coils rise from its crown. An early seismographic listening device, a long-range atmospheric Geiger counter, or a kind of antique transformer for the conversion of paranormal electricities—the mysterious purpose of design and function of the device, or mechanism,[75] brings a quintessentially Lynchian industrial[76] quality to this early twentieth-century *waiting room*; but is no doubt equipped with an ambient warning system specific to its preternatural sensitivities.

Minute 30

A medium close-up on Señorita Dido shows her *listening*, listening and waiting, in a dazzling high-collared gown against the clamshell sofa like a Weimar diva awaiting her call. The occasional digital skipping of the somnambulant prohibition jazz indicates, by that distinctive *Twin Peaks* cue, that the soundscape of this *place* may be happening in reverse and holding her in a kind of serene and contemplative loop. Until that morphine daze is interrupted by an aquatic and clamorous pinging of some kind of alarm. The Señorita in further close-up reveals little physical reaction to the sonic intrusion, but the subtlest registration of impending urgency in the sympathetic pools of her eyes. Perhaps the gravest urgency.

Minute 31

The bulbous black mechanism is flashing and clanging—and it is the Giant who responds to the alarm, or the Fireman as he will come to be called.[77] He enters the room from behind

FIGURE 5 Twin Peaks: The Return © *Showtime 2017.*

the device and examines it, making a small arc around it in his characteristically careful gait. Then he turns and silently convenes with his companion as if to say, "*It's happening now. We knew that it would.*"

He turns again *downstage,* as it were, glances at the pair of gauges, and then stands centerstage, spanning the frame from top to bottom, improbably taller than the device itself, gazing sternly toward the camera as a sentient Velazquez in the agency of his *Las Meninas*: the uncanny unity of a composition completing itself by looking back upon and including the observing audience in that composition. He's looking at us now, completing our astral projection across the purple nightsea.

A close-up clarifies that the Fireman is looking just *over* the camera, seeing past the screen, searching the window through which we'd entered—and with us, surely *time* has entered his house. He searches beyond us and across the purple sea for what terrible thing lay out there, yet arrived. The granite contours of his skull, the ceremonial dignity and station of his tuxedo and bowtie, the troubled brow of the gentle giant searching, the troubled brow of the Fireman searching fire.

Minute 32

All the while the dull clanging of the bell. He turns and bends to the pair of glass-covered gauges on the device, assessing their indications, then presses his finger to a button and switches off the repeating alert. He faces Señorita Dido again, sharing silent counsel once more, as if to say, "*It is happening. The sadness has come.*"

The composition of the parlor in the Fireman's home is exemplary of what Lynch describes as the contrasting *speed* of aesthetic qualities.[78] The great slowness and length of the Giant/Fireman himself bisecting the height of the room, the narcotic rapture of the seated Señorita, the matte and monochrome still-life of the black iron bell; amid the accelerated cacophony of the sitting room upholstery, wallpaper, and carpeted floor all vibrating about the metronomic disturbance of the alarm—a total collision of opposite optical speeds resulting in a highly rare and volatile state, the aesthetic chain reaction occurring inside a diorama particle accelerator. Lynch arranges the clashing furies of a theatrical cosmos swirling about the duck's eye[79] of a compositional hurricane and brings them into Calder-like balance, as the body of that duck, precariously balanced in space—strange, comedic, awkward, elegant, simultaneously dark and bright, and brimming with grace—a unifying temporal antidote to Virilio's speed of cosmic fear: the Fireman's house at the speed of optical harmony and kinetic tranquility.

The Fireman exits, leaving the Señorita alone within a laudanum of music[80] wafting through the sitting room, a languorous sanctum out-of-time. It is History-as-Apocalypse that has finally arrived on a shockwave of mythic pathos and cosmic terror,[81] the demiurgic doppelgänger of cosmic being and its legion of eschatological tulpas, or *characters* projected as the anthropomorphic menace by which that imposter force is directly perceived. The Black Lodge of Judy.

Minute 33

A grand staircase, ascending symmetrically to an upper lobby. The Fireman steadies himself along the bannister, the *backwards* soft-shoe of his steps sinking *upward* from the plush carpeting—his magical means of eliding linear time. The camera tilts with him up the stairs, beckoning us along.

A great hall, whorling in the marbled pattern of a flattened and frozen sea. Another large bell-shaped *device* stands to the side, rising from a pool of light and obscuring into a gorgeous chiaroscuro of Victorian noir. The Fireman enters from the shadowed recesses and crosses the open floor from background to foreground, pushing a wake of time toward the camera, his steps clipping in reverse and following him out of frame.

Minute 34

He climbs the stairs to a proscenium stage and stands before the antique, weathered screen of an early twentieth-century cinema.[82] Yet another bell-shaped electronic transformer occupies the corner of the stage—increasingly uncanny, as we really have no idea what they do, but in the alarming relay of their recurring, shadowed, and inanimate presence insinuate their cryptic purpose as some kind of paranormal conductor of eidetic energy, or the harnessing of *ideas*.[83]

Indeed, the Fireman raises his left hand, and the screen comes alive, activated by a gesture of telekinetic *hand-tracking* or the Victorian retro-future of a touch-free screen, our VR future now. He watches a replay of the preceding events in a 4:3 aspect ratio[84]—those events that apparently set off the alarm. He watches the Trinity sequence, flickering now in the light of 35mm projection, face open, eyes wide, searching the screen. He sees the Woodsmen scurrying about the filling station with increasing concern. And he witnesses *the experiment* expelling her foul somatic matter into the void, into the world. When the playback reaches the adult-embryonic face of Killer Bob, filling the center of the screen, it pauses.

Minute 35

The Fireman approaches the screen stage left, opposite the bell-shaped transformer to his stage right. He stands facing the house beside the paused and flickering[85] image of Bob. Then the gentle giant slowly levitates, standing straight as a pole and smoothly rising above the stage until he is floating at the top of the screen. The bright swelling and wistful ether of Badalamenti's synthetic theatre organ[86] accompanies the sequence of theatrical action before a silent film within a silent film—a kind of epic, silent opera.

Right on cue, Señorita Dido makes her entrance at the back of the theatre in the dramatic backlighting of a follow-spot and ceremoniously crosses the house floor.

Minute 36

The projected image of Killer Bob looms large on the screen and the Señorita approaches with the liturgical poise of a bride walking to the alter, her great shadow preceding her. She ascends to the stage in the bright pool of spotlight, she and her silhouette, where the Fireman is now floating like a corpse at an angle to the screen. A small cloud of *gold* appears at the top of the Fireman's head—the only occurrence of color in the scene—and the cinema screen is then filled with stars, a galaxy of stars upon the night sky.

Minute 37

The cloud of *color* develops into an emission of gold dust swarming from the top of the Fireman's head against the silver screen scene, he gently levitating as a vessel in corpse pose. Dido stands before the screen of stars, gazing up in wonder and exhilaration. The Fireman's eyes are wide awake, in trance, golden stardust streaming from his head as a kind of celestial antithesis to *the experiment's* visceral spew, and mingling with stars from the screen as they are drawn toward it, crossing a cinematic threshold in which the fourth wall is not an artifice for the suspension of disbelief but a membrane conducting the transmission of a poetic real as two-way communication.

Minute 38

A microcosmos of golden starlight pouring from the Fireman's consciousness and assembling into some kind of extracorporeal nervous system, a stellar uterine form—and we are racing with stars in the black and golden night alight. Señorita Dido standing rapt and gorgeous in the strobing projection of electric white light as a ball of gold is produced from the center of the Fireman's pineal galaxy, a golden orb in counterpoint to the tumorous spore of Killer Bob. The golden sphere[87] descends in an arc

Minute 39

into the outstretched hands of Señorita Dido. She holds it before her, lovingly, as a glowing and weightless bowling ball—and it contains the *future* face of *Twin Peaks* senior prom queen Laura Palmer, preserved as a holographic icon in the radiant amber of *1989*,[88] an impossible Christmas ornament of the angelic devastation of Laura. The Señorita brings the radiant visage to her lips and holds the girl in blessing for as long as she is able, by the simplest means of which we are capable, and then releases her into Badalamenti's soaring cathedral.

FIGURE 6 Twin Peaks: The Return © *Showtime 2017.*

Minute 40

A clockwork of golden gears and abacuses is suspended from the ceiling above the proscenium stage, and two gold discuses, shallow-belled terminals presumably connected to the mysterious black bell transformer also powering the screen— all setting in motion a great axial arm curving into a golden horn.[89]

The golden sphere of Laura ascends into the bell of the horn, passing through the corpus of the *instrument* as it rotates toward the movie screen, stars racing us now toward a mid-century black-and-white newsreel animation of *Planet Earth* flickering into view upon the cinematic television. The orb of Laura[90] exits the mouthpiece end of the horn as a viscous droplet of gold, for a moment pressing and flattening against the surface tension of the screen itself (a marvelous tactile detail) and then releasing *into* the screen, briefly color matching to its black-and-white TV context before turning gold again and descending toward North America, or the period simulation of *this Earth* in its proto-telegenic state.

A master shot finally reveals the full set piece of Lynch's theatre,[91] shot on-location at the Los Angeles Tower Theatre.[92] A giant iron-black bell-device rises from the floor of the black-and-white hall, its cathode terminals connected to cables ascending to the upper reaches of the theatre; another smaller device on stage. Señorita Dido stands center stage in her spotlight before an early televisual representation of the globe's Western Hemisphere, the golden orb of Laura Palmer descending toward the American southwest, or Texas.[93] Above the screen, the golden horn of the golden clockworks, and beside it, floating in repose, the Fireman *streaming* his sentient cosmos of golden stardust. The total mechanism of the cinematic composition here is as a great *theatrical seeing apparatus*, the vintage prototype of a two-way, interactive clairvoyance-device, a contraption contemporaneous with the otherworldly (globally) weaponized *magic* of the atomic *gadget.* But a seeing device at *human* scale, an anachronistic human physicality, or human theatricality in contrast to the nano-circuitry of our own contemporary device-seeing. And an elation of theatrical optics at this scale of human, presaging the ubiquitous panopticon voodoo of our own all-consuming visually augmented, temporally disorienting, geography-defying contemporary experience at the scale of algorithm, and the gleaming black-glass eye of the entity— the omniscient, networked, aluminosilicate *experiment* of our own world. Here, we see by the magnifying fresnel vitrine of a great cinematic lens: *the holographic apparatus of the world as symbolic field*—the stained-glass carnal church of David Lynch. *Telling time.*

Minute 41

A hollow wind. An arid wind. Fade in on a desert dune at night, rippled with windscape, yet black and white. The on-screen clock counts forward with a distinctly mid-century mechanical click: *1945, 1946, 1947, 1948, 1949, 1950, 1951, 1952, 1953, 1954, 1955*

1956
AUGUST 5
NEW MEXICO DESERT

With each and every setup in *The Return,* Lynch defies expectation of his own visual vernacular—his own style—by enfolding yet another angle of the world into the Lynchian.[94] Here, a five-shot suite of the desert sand, each a lunar still, modernist in rhythm and contrast. Edward Weston, Antonioni, O'Keefe. The fourth shot lands on the *speckled egg,* the egg jettisoned from *the experiment's* production to rest upon a washboard of desert crust in the moonlit night.

When the egg begins to hatch, we jump to a medium close-up.

Minute 42

A creature hatches from the egg, with all the isolated aural detail of a *hatching*[95]—crisp, existential ASMR[96] dread, flaking and fluid, with a membranous squelching of rupturing mucus. The hatchling pulls itself forth and frees itself from the infra-stellar eggshell with a slightly croaking chirp and vigorously flutters its wings for the first time. Neither the outer space alien invasion of H. G. Wells (and all to follow); nor Spielberg's teleological humanoid as Jungian super-projection; nor a Roswell Grey escaping from some government black site into the New Mexico desert; but a creaturely mutation native to our own pathological morphology—an ambiguous *familiar* of ambiguous intent from some atomic *interior elsewhere*: it is the now-infamous hatchling, or *frogmoth*, a kind of locust amphibian with a frog's hind legs and abdomen, and the upper torso of a flying insect rendered in the truly uncanny artifice of a tactile 1990s-inflected CGI. It is a technique employed across *The Return*—integrating cinematic object with the artistry of its artificial animation: what it is, and how it's made, as twin strands of its own aesthetic DNA. The effect (as with Trinity, or the "evolution of the arm" as tree) is of discovering that uncanny species as being endemic to its native habitat: the Lynchian. The uncanny valley is reestablished as a real geography, reorienting us to its own hyper-contemporary, artificially intelligent terms in such a way that does not require *believability* at all but exists as its own ontological field of beings, its own morphology of psychic lifeforms; in the case of the frogmoth, a kind of reanimated meme or *animal* that has sprung from the real primordial soup of the mutated noospheric climate of a weaponized globe.

The creature drags itself in a small arc around the egg and across the desert floor and riffles off into the night.

Minute 43

A full moon, passing of clouds in the monochrome moonlight.
"Did you like that song?"
"Yes. I did like that song."
It is the first dialogue that we've heard in over twenty-six minutes, since the countdown to the Trinity Test. A pedestrian structure, jolting in its own way, and comforting, after all that we've seen and, quite literally, all that we've been through. Human voices, as their own kind of extraordinary strangeness now. A pair of teenagers, walking in the night. They round the corner from behind a gas station and pass before it along a rural dirt road. Well-dressed in a flounced crinoline dress, bobby socks, and sweater; a white button-down shirt and dark jacket recently out-grown in the sleeves—a *boy* and a *girl* out for a formal stroll along the darkness on the edge of town, on the frontier hinterlands of a Hollywood that never arrives, and has already passed them by. Douglas Sirk, Nicholas Ray. All the open night of the clear desert air before them, an expanse of impossible future promised by the facade of impossible constructs *imprinted by power*: The promise of a future that

FIGURE 7 Twin Peaks: The Return © *Showtime 2017.*

the intervention of history—and of *world*—yet conspires with every novel cruelty to disallow. But inside it they walk, smiling bashfully. Shining.

"Look! I found a penny! Oh . . . And it's head's up. That means it's good luck."

"I hope it does bring you good luck."

Minute 44

A dim vista of desert scrub in that same night. The silhouette of a man appears *in the air*, descending out of a thin overcast haze. He floats to the ground, landing gently as a phantom, and walks toward us as inky shadow. Another angle on that same desert basin, and a second spectral man appears, crunching toward us in the feral night.

Cut now to the interior of a vehicle looking out through a vintage split windshield rolling down a nearby desert road. Headlights up ahead in the oncoming lane. The car slows down and stops, as figures are visible entering the road.

Woodsmen.

Minute 45

Alarmed, an impeccable 1950s-styled couple peers out into the night beyond the windshield and over the hood and the headlights and the gleaming chrome of the grill as a Woodsman approaches their vehicle. Camera in first-person now, from the point of view of the encroaching Woodsmen himself, lumbering and handheld—a character perspective employed by Lynch only very selectively, and here perhaps as yet seeing out from the interior of that *A-bomb* by which he arrived, all charcoaled and charred and now crackling with the static and gravel of some smoldering malpaís, he approaches the travelers' roadster

FIGURE 8 Twin Peaks: The Return © *Showtime* 2017.

as though *they* are the guinea pig interlopers from some test-market halcyon plan now crossing his own land of fire.

The driver opens his door but then pauses as the Woodsman leans into the open window wearing a blackened Shenandoah, Amish-style beard, a filthy flannel shirt, and a winter trapper's hat, his face and his neck and his ears all coal-fired black as though he'd walked right out of the blast furnace engine, the smoking engine room of Trinity itself, and he its smoking engineer now walking right up to their car holding a long rolled cigarette out before him in his hand, the Woodsman asks but one thing.

"Gotta light?"
"Gotta light?"
"Gotta light?"

Another Woodsman looks on, leaning in over the hood, and the lady of the vehicle howls a guttural, slow-motion yowl as her husband tries to work out what's happening—*tries to see what he's seeing*—in the interrogation of some strobing exterior glare.

"Gotta light?"
"Gotta light?"
"Gotta light?"

Minute 46

Then he lays on the gas, squealing his tires as he swerves around another Woodsman in the road and tears away. With focus pulled to the couple from a backseat camera position, husband and wife are now illuminated in noir silhouette by the dashboard light as terrified extras in a Hitchcock film *at a drive-in screening of a Hitchcock film* beyond their windshield: the blurring, postwar lost highway racing toward them.

Meanwhile—mirroring them oppositely, in both age and trajectory—the younger couple continue their stroll *toward us* and converse in halting, adolescent courtship dialogue, venturing the space between them with the schoolbook words in their possession.

"*So . . . I thought you were going with Mary.*"

"*No. No, that's over.*"

"*Are you . . . sad . . . about that?*"

"*No.*"

It's a trope, or cliché, for which *Twin Peaks* is well-known—teenage courtship dialogue, enfolding itself as a kind of thrilling taboo—now finally located at the origin of its source, in the searing aurora of the atomic age. In the night of the hunter.

Minute 47

When they reach the girl's house, she thanks him for walking her home. He asks permission to kiss her. She is unsure, indicating she might not be ready for that. "*Please,*" he says. "*Just one?*" She smiles and closes her eyes. He steps forward and leans in and kisses her sweetly. She exhales, turns, and walks away, leaving him glowing.

Minute 48

From the height of the front porch, she pauses in the porchlight and waves goodbye, smiling down at the boy, then she darts inside her house and closes the front door. In another mirroring match cut, the Woodsman climbs a low desert rise and looks out upon a squat cinderblock building beneath a communications antenna rising against the darkened hills and then tramps down a two-track service road snaking toward the compound.

Minute 49

When the twilight is gone
And no songbirds are singing
When the twilight is gone
You come into my heart

A tenor voice calling out, clear as a bell from the KPJK rural radio station.[97] A vinyl 45 single of *The Platters* is spinning on the turntable and crackling softly over the airwaves. It's 10:16 p.m. according to the clock on the sound-booth wall. A disc jockey seated at the classic console quietly reviews a binder of his broadcast programming.

And here in my heart you will stay
While I pray

With great care, Lynch then builds a compact montage on the receiving end of those spellbinding airwaves. A vintage radio glowing from the tool bench of an auto garage, the night mechanic at work in the glow of a work light under the hood of a classic pickup. A middle-aged waitress is wiping down the long U-shaped lunch counter at a diner after hours, alone with a long day's end. And *the girl*, now folded upon her bed in a printed nightdress before the floral wallpaper and lace curtains of her bedroom, lost in melodic reverie over the evening's sweet encounter. Three brief, perfectly framed, and gorgeously lit black-and-white scenes, believably crafted in action and design, triangulating the Arcadian ethos of a peaceable Rockwell society at work and at rest, Americans alone in the shared euphoria of an infrastructural mythos, a moment of ruminative emptiness tuned to the Billboard lullaby of *My Prayer.* Desolation angels incandescent in the ghost light.

My prayer is to linger with you
At the end of the day
In a dream that's divine

And then the Woodsman arrives—emerging from the long shadow cast in the blindspot of that holographic national monument. He walks out of the badlands, passing before a spiny ocotillo juxtaposed against the computational score of decorative glass bricks curving along the outer wall of the radio station, a blank periodic table translucent between human beings and the unforeseeably algorithmic future swarming with reaper drones and memes.

Minute 50

He walks through the front doors of the radio station like a rogue and miscreant salesman with no bibles to sell but the smoking black magic of language itself. The receptionist turns from her filing cabinets with a smile, but that effusive American hospitality quickly drains away.

"Gotta light?"

He steps toward her—long, white cigarette dangling from his blackened, bearded face; and she is simultaneously drawn to him, her fingers and open wrist presenting strangely, leading her hips and rapturous expression of horror in a slow-motion fatal attraction toward libidinous inevitability: an external force, or confluence of opposing forces, acting upon their bodies colliding beyond individual will. He reaches out his blackened hand, woolen in a frontiersman's fingerless glove, and as a laying on of hands, places it on her head. Then impassively and seemingly without effort but to her willing cries and the grounding of some great telluric force, he sinks her to her knees—*camera shaking furiously, blood pouring down her face to* My Prayer— and baptismally crushes her skull. On the R&B downbeat of her body flopping to the floor, he turns his attention to the sound-booth window and the disc jockey there within.

"Gotta light?"

Minute 51

The deejay swivels in his chair to confront the dark silhouette of a hand reaching toward him and then laid upon the headphones on his crown. He grimaces in agony in shirtsleeves and a necktie beneath the intruder's fatal grip, RCA broadcast microphone hanging before him under the KPJK call letters.

The Woodsman swipes his free hand across the spinning 45, screeching the needle across vinyl—an abrupt and violent rupture resounding through the mechanic's night garage, the waitress' empty counter, the girl's teenage bedroom, each of them turning their attention to the sudden current of static in the void. The Woodsman flips a switch on the control panel, an

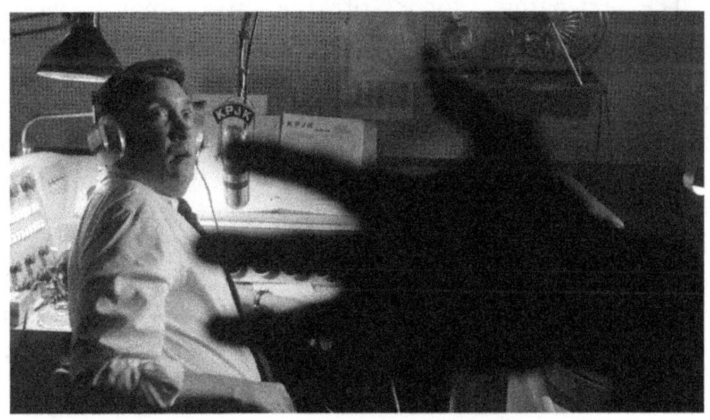

FIGURE 9 Twin Peaks: The Return © *Showtime* 2017.

action performed decisively and with impunity, like he knows just what to do. He therewith takes up the microphone and draws it to him and delivers unto his listeners a poem.

"*This is the water, and this is the well. Drink full and descend. The horse is the white of the eyes, and dark within.*"

The whites of his own Woodsman eyes glistening through bitumen greasepaint toward some horizon printed of infernal method, unlit cigarette still dangling from his mouth, KPJK microphone cradled before him.

"*This is the water, and this is the well. Drink full and descend. The horse is the white of the eyes, and dark within.*"

Minute 52

The skull of the station's disc jockey begins to crack and collapse under the pressure of the Woodsman's brimstone hand. The waitress hears his on-air address, swooning as she wipes down the countertop and collapses behind the bar. *This is the water, and this is the well. Drink full and descend.* The mechanic's wrench falls from his hand, clanging to the concrete floor, and he too cannot withstand. *The horse is the white of the eyes.*

The telepathic force of the Woodsman's words incapacitating his listeners and rendering them unconscious—a dark counterpart to the primal euphoria or frenzy-inducing capabilities of R&B and rock & roll music amplified by *electric* means. A spell cast via modern communications technology, hijacked by some rogue poet-terrorist and encoded somewhere in the ambiguity of its meaning—*a terrorism as the ambiguity of meaning*—in which the meaning of the poem is sourced to the intended physiological effect: to render unconscious. A malevolent transmission of the disorienting artistry of poetic language disseminated at scale. *And dark within.*

Less than a year before the streaming premiere of Part 8 *Gotta Light?* there was a parallel upheaval of the means and meaning and architecture of communication, and a corresponding shockwave of networked neural hysteria—*an emergency of language*[98]—preempting the Woodsman's 2017 anesthetizing poem. In October of 2016, Bob Dylan was awarded the Nobel Prize in Literature; and one month later, by the gales of November, an American president was elected on the performative strategy of catalyzing and accelerating that emergency of language. The performance poet and the *performer of reality,* each of them in their own way masters of the extraordinarily liquid and vernacular capabilities of language; one in the service of language itself, the other in the service of himself and the power he would gather by its voodoo—and something of each of them evoked in the Woodsman.

Dylan, a modernist, surrealist, Dadaist, and astonishingly prolific lyricist, is perhaps most importantly (to the unorthodoxy of the Nobel selection) a vocalist, whose literature was his very incantation of it—its *delivery*; a category-annihilating artist who by being awarded literature's highest accolade briefly annihilated it as well. The repeating, sepulchral lines of the Woodsman's brief poem recall the haunting surrealism of Dylan's masterpiece *A Hard Rain's A-Gonna Fall,* sensitively delivered by Patti Smith at the Nobel ceremony—

"I saw a white ladder all covered with water . . .
I met a young child beside a dead pony . . .
And the executioner's face is always well hidden . . .
Where black is the color, where none is the number."[99]

—a lyric itself indebted to Allen Ginsberg's *Howl* published in 1956, the very year of the Woodsman's pirate broadcast: "What sphinx of cement and aluminum bashed open their skulls and ate up their brains and imagination?"[100] A devotional disorientation of the senses unto illumination.

The forty-fifth and forty-seventh[101] president of the United States, alternately, deploys a kind of sustained poetic terrorism—a communication of disorientation, and a clarity of disorientation in which the disorientation is the intent, the contradictory performance of a shambolic precision. Language as spell, intent on weaponizing communication itself into a compass-scrambling electromagnetic pulse, amplified by the unprecedented array of participatory communication technologies at an unprecedented scale, the intimately global scale of the internet.[102]

Amid the legion of discharging Trumpisms, the mini-poetic list "Person, Woman, Man, Camera, TV." was particularly derided, and particularly meme-able. It had a ring to it. And a meter, not altogether uncommon as the contemporary literature trend of the listicle or the list poem. But in its contextual (presidential) absurdity, "Person, Woman, Man, Camera, TV." merits intertextual comparison to the famous Chomsky sentence "Colorless green ideas sleep furiously," a sentence invented by linguist Noam Chomsky "as an example of a sentence that is grammatically well-formed but semantically non-sensical. There is no obvious, understandable meaning that can be derived from it, which demonstrates the distinction between syntax and semantics and the idea that a syntactically well-formed sentence is not guaranteed to also be semantically well-formed."[103] Or, not guaranteed to mean anything at all. Sentences, or artfully strung sequences of words, may appear to have meaning, but do not. Or they may appear to have no meaning and purpose at all when in fact they do—covertly.

Person, Woman, Man, Camera, TV.

Colorless green ideas sleep furiously.

The para-speech vernacular of the former-future president quite often seems to meet the criterion of the Chomsky sentence: grammatically functional yet semantically nonsensical, and vice versa. Yet that functionality—as with the Woodsman's poem—is itself entirely severed from its meaning and serves quite another purpose altogether: it is not what (Trump) says as a political performer that matters, but the scale at which what is said is disruptive to syntactical and semiotic meaning alike. Take *Covfefe*. A meaningless transmission that could have been spoken by the arm himself, inside the *Twin Peaks* waiting room: backwards sounding, or perhaps even inside out, endowed and encoded with mimetic magic—not meaning, but *value*—by the total disruption of narrative itself. Its radical ambiguity is its functionality, its value, effective to the extent that it is disruptive to meaning—at scale. Language must be trusted in order for it to hold meaning. Here, its functional value is its ability to subvert all trust. The cognitive crudity and ultimately injurious cruelty of the so-called Trump *weave* operates as its own kind of signal-jam, the magnetic field of an oligarch's sycophancy, powered by the luxuriance of one who does not even require language at all, but in which it is rather outsourced as the *performance* of language, the replicant sentience of a ChatGPT generating mnemonic key chains for crypto accounts—or nuclear codes—as inhuman speech.

The symbiosis between the Trumpian vernacular and the prosthetic appendage of its radically inhuman amplification is no longer a means of communication at all but a networked encounter so vastly out-scaling preexisting human social relations as to constitute a nervous system-regulating apparatus, a cybernetic organism with all the malevolent ambiguity of a conspiratorial order. The president of the most powerful country on earth, amplified by the algorithmic infrastructure (or so-called social media) of the wealthiest man on earth can no longer even be considered to be human, but an algorithmic entity whose speech cannot be considered according to the parameters of free speech because it violates the very parameters of human speech. Its electro-semiotic impact on actual humans is to render all communication as a code-scrambling metadata—as colorless green ideas sleep furiously—in which it makes no difference at all whether what is spoken is true, or has any sense or meaning, or has ever even actually been said. A conspiracy of narrative in which language is not utilized as a vehicle for the transportation and communication of information but as a means of inducing disequilibrium; as if by the broadcasting of some vastly networked spell, a neurological disruption renders its recipients unconscious so that some other parasitic force may enter. A stranger comes to town. Whistling a tinsel tune. The showman as shaman.[104] *Drink full and descend.*

Out of the scorched and razed frontier of its own interior, that stranger arrives with another song in mind. Inside the historically fictional 1956 of a fictionally infused 2017, the Woodsman comes crossing a bridge of fire, calling across the vestigial chasm of a corpus callosum fried, before the congregation of a collective bicameral mind, assembled and fervent to hear from subatomic God himself, when it is God's blacksmith who rises scraped and forged from the blast-waste of Trinity as a populist demon, an automaton-Dylan forged of sulfurous mudpot clay canting scripture summoned directly from the id of the cultural economy, from the great smoking pit at the core of the country communicating exactly where we are—a set of coordinates radiating in blank verse. The Woodsman speaking in black ink smoke.

This is the water, and this is the well. Drink full and descend. The horse is the white of the eyes, and dark within.

On the outskirts of town the frogmoth newly hatched from its egg drags itself across the crusted ground, pushing itself forward by the fleshy musculature of its hind legs and guiding itself along with six arthropod appendages.

Minute 53

This is the water, and this is the well. Drink full and descend. The girl lies down on her bed, radio near her head, and is comfortably put to sleep. *The horse is the white of the eyes, and dark within.*

Outside—the frogmoth approaches her bedroom window ajar to the night's light breeze. The creature flutters and hops twice, leaping into a heavy hover, legs dangling beneath it and whirring in first flight to a clumsy landing upon the windowsill, and heaves itself inside.

Minute 54

The frogmoth moves more easily across the smoothed sheet of the girl's bed and crawls right up to her face, sleeping serene—as we will never see her again. For she is a thirteen-year-old Sarah Novak, who will marry Leland Palmer and become Sarah Palmer, the mother of Laura, and whose father worked for a time with the Manhattan Project at Los Alamos.[105] Crouched before her now, we see that the frogmoth animal is quite big, the size of a very large mouse. It raises up on its front legs, and with its proboscis purrs into her mouth. She responds without stirring by opening her mouth wide, and the creature crawls inside, probing the rim of her lips with its six insect legs and then burrowing into the cavity of her, wings folding and quivering, hind legs extending and then gently clawing for purchase and we see that the frog's legs do not terminate in an amphibian's webbed feet, but in two tiny five-fingered hands, withdrawing slowly as two arms retreating into her mouth and disappearing inside, a Hieronymus Bosch crossover species migrating from one painting to another, from *The Garden of Earthly Delights*

FIGURE 10 Twin Peaks: The Return © *Showtime 2017*.

to the metamorphic viscera of *Twin Peaks*, where it will occupy and inhabit Sarah Palmer as a symbiote, feeding on the devouring hollow of her future-trauma: the incestuous and devastating domestic legacy of Trinity as a haunted, looping mutation. Sarah Palmer, empath, open nerve-node, lightning rod. She will fracture and shatter in time. She will suffer the insult and daily agony, the glitching cognitive dissonance of a culture living out the fugue state of its own psychotic production; the simultaneity of its nightmare organized into some kind of horrific livability, a post-apocalyptic survivalism as the mimicry of a nuclear family—the dissociative fissure of a society forced to simulate itself as bad actors. Bad actors in a green-screened antechamber to the excruciating false binary of its black-and-white lodges, forever unresolved.

The absurdist reality-choreography of actors on a TV show inside a TV show who don't even know that they are actors at all,[106] but are rather a kind of malevolent stupidity[107] as soap opera dramaturgy, the cancerous and saccharine social performance necessitated by an absence of the conspiratorial backstory that they have been denied—the redacted crimes of their own freakish engineering, as if the characters themselves were in possession of an autonomic agency, an algorithmic sentience inside the diorama of the television in the museum of the present. Feral animatronic animals in a state of unconscious agitation before the fibrillating tremors of a coming earthquake. A great machine-moon is coming over the horizon, one that would ultimately collapse observer and observed into the real estate of a radiating cinematic object. A crystal ball, a black star, a death star, a space mountain. Thus we are the content. The metadata itself. While the bona fide script is eternally waited for, the grotesquerie of the sideshow goes on as the main event, as if the narrative power of our age has been outsourced to porn stars incubating the predatory cryptid. She closes her mouth and swallows[108]—all the while the spoken words of the Woodsman's chant.

This is the water, and this is the well. Drink full and descend. The horse is the white of the eyes, and dark within.

This is the water, and this is the well. Drink full and descend. The horse is the white of the eyes, and dark within.

Minute 55

Inside the radio station studio, the Woodsman clenches down on his unlit cigarette and clamps down on the disc jockey's head. An excruciating pressure of mewling and crackling of bone, fingers digging into the radioman's scalp with tectonic force and ferocity in the whites of his eyes—crushing his skull. Thick black blood pouring from the back of the fractured head of matted hair and headphones, spilling and splatting to the floor in a gleaming black-and-white splattering of props department brains and blood. He withdraws his fingers from inside the deejay's shattered cranium and exits the studio, leaving his earworm apocrypha behind, an apocalypse of words having served their purpose now inscribed as archival interference winding through the grain of unconscious night.

Minute 56

The Woodsman walks back out through the front doors of the radio station, thunderquake rumbling of his exit, a storm coming on the blind horizon, heat lightning flashing on the cinematic threshold between horror, melodrama, naturalism, western, and electric noir, and he walks off into that night beyond the perimeter halo of light, beyond the outpost of the known and laminate world, and disappears beyond the rim of it, vanishing in the dark, inside the pooling night. Out there to meet them.

Horses out there, whinnying in the dark. Ghost white horses in the eye of their absolute absence. Of the night turned inside out.

Horses out there, whinnying.

Horses inside the country.

Horses out there, whinnying in the dark.

Horses out there, whinnying in the dark.

Postscript

The Owl in Daylight

There are sentences that come in the night, as black smoke curling inside the dark. In the morning they are gone. I never saw them but I know that they were there.

Like the owls that come up the valley to the eucalyptus tree outside my window. I lay awake listening to them calling out to each other like a telegraph. Beyond, the booming sea.

And when I hear them they save me. How do they do that? How do the owls save me?

They give me courage.

Jeff Wood
January 16, 2025[1]
Portugal

NOTES

Introduction

1 That is, the auction house trailer park trinket *Balloon Dog* or the menacing and whimsically oversized Chia Pet *Puppy*.

2 The map of the country itself reads as a Maya Lin-style wall of memorial place names to Native America.

3 And where, forty-four years later, my own son Cooper would see *Star Wars* for the first time on *his* seventh birthday.

4 A Trojan Horse (or Imperial AT-AT Walker) that consumes rather than regurgitates—its emptiness is its enzymatic weapon, as a stomach turned inside out, the world digesting itself.

5 And its narrative counterpart, the *deus ex machina*.

6 "All of my work is directed against those who are bent, through stupidity or design, on blowing up the planet or rendering it uninhabitable," declared Burroughs in a 1965 interview with *The Paris Review*.

7 Paul Virilio, *The Administration of Fear* (Semiotext(e), 2012), 9.

8 Virilio, *The Administration of Fear*, 22.

9 Virilio, *The Administration of Fear*, 35.

10 Virilio, *The Administration of Fear*, 32.

11 Virilio, *The Administration of Fear*, 55.

12 Virilio, *The Administration of Fear*, 63.

13 Virilio, *The Administration of Fear*, 75.

14 What the entrepreneurs of *wellness* capitalize on as adrenal and cortisol fatigue.

15 Virilio, *The Administration of Fear*, 35.

16 See *The Removals*, written and directed by Nick Rombes (Two Dollar Radio, 2016).

17 These in addition to those early encounters with cinematic roadside text as some kind of prototype for an incorporeal sentient *voice* or malevolent AI, the metadata of HELL IS REAL incanting in the night and in broad daylight.

18 After Italo Calvino's aesthetic "Multiplicity" in *Six Memos for the Next Millennium.*

19 *It's happening again.*

20 ^^ When in fact the world *has* ended, but carries on as the fraudulent imposter of itself, as the symptom of our own suspicion. The problem is—when? When did the world end? What year is this?

21 Virilio, *The Administration of Fear*, 78.

Minutes 1–56

1 The third installment of which, *Return of the Jedi*, Lynch was astonishingly (after *Eraserhead* and *The Elephant Man*) invited to direct by George Lucas himself.

2 *"If you strike me down, I shall become more powerful than you can possibly imagine."* —Obi-Wan Kenobi

3 A two-way semiosis demonstrated to great effect in Cormac McCarthy's *The Road*: the taste-sensation of the *Coca-Cola* as much an artifact as the design of the container and logo themselves, both communicated and summoned in the reader as each other, as a unity, in a landscape devoid of both flavor and color, a world devoid of design.

4 I think briefly, too, of the Overlook Hotel, Bates Motel, and the mythic legacy of the American hotel, on-screen and off, as a brooding protagonist, not haunted, per se, but possessing of a mercurial omniscience on the haunted field of the American landscape—a container of souls, its own haunted subjectivity compounded from the souls of its collective guests, vulnerable to its architecture. And of course the natural inclination in the animation of houses is toward the diabolical. A thing at

rest is a trustworthy thing, but a house in possession of an anthropomorphism is a house possessed. The cinematic list is long, but among them, the Palmer House is supreme.

5   *"What year is this?"*

6   The white disc with the black dot center curiously signaling something that we will hear later in the timecode but much earlier in the timeline: *The horse is the white of the eyes and dark within.*

7   The first solar eclipse to cross the entire continental United States in 100 years. August 21, 2017.

8   The first picture ever taken of an actual black hole, an image captured using eight radio telescopes around the globe, essentially converting the Earth itself into a giant camera, or an arachnid seeing apparatus. April 17, 2017.

9   *The Kekulé Problem* was published on April 17, 2017, the same day as the photo taken of M87*, the first-ever image of a black hole. This illumination of a cosmic darkness and McCarthy's essay on the origin of language each explore the extreme and opposing limits of representation, converging on the dark matter of *Twin Peaks: The Return*. The dark machine at the center of the world.

10   And that the red-curtained waiting room is also The Black Lodge even though it is also not.

11   *"Something is happening, isn't it, Margaret?"*

12   Cormac McCarthy, "The Kekulé Problem; Where did language come from?" *Nautilus*. April 17, 2017.

13   Cormac McCarthy, *Blood Meridian; or The Evening Redness in the West* (Random House, 1985), 20.

14   @loved_orleer

15   And with its 1991 *Terminator 2: Judgement Day*, a major entry into the apocalyptic canon with its shocking nuclear holocaust scene at a playground full of children.

16   A spectacular Rutger Hauer performing perhaps the most sublime and moving death soliloquy ever put on film, a monologue delivered by an inhuman replicant reflectively performing the death of a human as the memorial moment of his own sentient death, or termination. Roy's monologue is

itself reminiscent of the "death" dialogue performed by HAL, perhaps the earliest records of an emergent canon of AI self-eulogizing.

17   And in further prescient world-bleeding, MacLachlan's Bad Cooper resembles even the twin multibillionaire tech-oligarchs of America, in skin tone, manner, and malevolence. Or rather the inverse: they, in gothic wigs, resemble him.

18   The supreme example of this Lynchian technique, of course, is, *"I'll fuck anything that moves!"* declared psychotically by Dennis Hopper's Frank Booth in *Blue Velvet*.

19   Frank Guan. "What Does David Lynch Have to Say About Race?" *Vulture*, September 12, 2017.

20   And as I will say over and over again, a cinema metamorphosed into content device.

21   There is a scene in Part 11 of *The Return* that is among Lynch's most bonkers, didactic, and devastating—a scene that is many things, yet is quite simply staged. A drive-by shooting occurs at the Double R Diner. Officer Bobby Briggs exits the diner to investigate. The random shooting was committed by a boy in a passing vehicle. He had found his father's firearm on the floor of the vehicle and fired it toward the diner. As Bobby assesses the situation, he notices that the boy, perhaps ten or eleven, and his father are dressed identically in camo hunting clothes. They are defiantly unapologetic for the shooting and the obvious parental negligence with regard to firearm possession—father and son affecting identical defiant and macho postures as a mode of Second Amendment cosplay. Meanwhile, a woman behind them won't stop honking her horn and screaming. Next to her, in the passenger seat, sits a zombie child spewing green bile. All of this in the prior context of Bobby's own family repeating its history of dysfunction, addiction, and self-destruction, a remarkably compound scene of specifically American social dysfunction staged as an over-the-top didactic surrealism—just a few years before the Kyle Rittenhouse shootings and landmark exoneration. The citizen security cosplay of a Martial Identity Agenda which seeks to weaponize all space as real estate by eliminating public space. The scene is devastating, and alongside the Trinity Test, will

come to occupy the very center of *The Return* as experimental American melodrama.

22 *"I am the FBI,"* Cooper will declare.

23 Guan, "What Does David Lynch Have To Say About Race."

24 @hering_david. David Hering. ". . . of great, childlike beauty and almost incomprehensible evil, both of which spring directly from the home (the house and the nation). He made it clear in his masterpiece, *Twin Peaks* (2017), that he saw the A-Bomb as the midwife of all American culture that came after. From death there comes beauty, but the beauty is never inextricable from the source of death. The undertow of this enmeshment is a deep, deep sadness that suffuses everything, one that runs through the entire work. He absorbs into this the US cultural adoption in the 1950s/60s of . . ." X, August 30, 2024, 8:26 p.m., https://x.com/hering_david/status/1820541916485673354.

25 ^^

26 *"Through the darkness of futures past, the magician longs to see. One chants out between two worlds, fire walk with me."*

27 Itself a great enucleated eyeball gouged from the ground and lying Lynchian as a severed ear among the weeds of the abandoned lot, molding and psychotropic as the contents of that plundered Longaberger Basket Building, strewn and thermoluminescent upon the cataclysmic landscape.

28 David Samuels, "Already Gone," *County Highway*, Vol. 2, Issue 4, January 2025.

29 The Sphere is everywhere now—as all of space flatlining into the neurological content of a total real estate. The globe of this great Earth is flattening into a glitching disc, everywhere we turn, the flat circle at the end of temporal geography, razed and smoothed by Trinity itself into a landscape looping as mirror. The world as uncanny double. The replicant real—everywhere. The uncanny valley is flattening entirely now, flattening into a spectral plane—this land of agents and ghouls. As the capacity for ambiguity is erased, the use-value of empathy is obliterated, and replaced by its replicant counterparts: algorithmic derangement and delirium; and in the space of that algorithmic delirium—that derangement as

faith—the earth is yet flat again. Flat circle as glitching mirror. Reality itself as phantasmagoric object, gridded and pixelated into units of possession. The world as holographic NFT. Snow globes and magnets for the refrigerators of oligarchs.

30 Paglen's Tor-networked museum piece *Autonomy Cube* also shares resonance with the transparent glass box in *The Return*'s Part 1; and his astonishing *Trinity Cube*, comprised of Trinitite, or Alamogordo glass, recovered from the Trinity Site and installed inside the Fukushima Exclusion Zone, might be imagined as an essential distillation of the entire substance of *The Return* as a super-density—the goopy, high-viscosity, napalm-grade garmonbozia of lethal American pathos congealed into a marbled, hard-candy block of sculpted mineral voodoo—Trinitite, the extraordinary mineral that may also very well comprise the core symbol of the *Twin Peaks* iconography: the owl ring.

31 A signature feature of nuclear test imagery, smoke trails are generated by rockets launched seconds before detonation as a technique for measuring blast front progression on film after the event. They were in fact not present at the Trinity Test. Here, an oversight, or more likely an added touch in the calibration of a hyperrealism.

32 Like the tiny Icelandic volcano erupting live at my desk all the through Covid winter lockdown as a streaming flatscreen snow globe.

33 And its 1984 BBC counterpart *Threads*.

34 A vast Area 51, or Zone, the exact dimensions of the country. The inevitable wave cancellation of Florida notwithstanding.

35 ^^

36 See pages 115–16 of Cormac McCarthy, *The Passenger* (Alfred A. Knopf, 2022).

37 McCarthy, *Blood Meridian*, 259.

38 Elsewhere in *The Return*, it is revealed that deputy director of the FBI, Gordon Cole, played by Lynch himself, has two large images featured prominently on his Bureau office walls, facing each other from opposite sides of the room: a massive photo of a mushroom cloud behind his desk, looming over Cole and

all who enter, and a portrait of Franz Kafka opposite, gazing at Cole/Lynch himself. Here, two towering iconographic poles converging on the bureaucratic apparatus of the entire twentieth century and the legacy of its ambient futurity yet to come.

39 An ecstatic truth perhaps most profoundly exemplified by Joshua Oppenheimer's *The Act of Killing*, a film produced by Herzog, which alongside Jonathan Glazer's *Zone of Interest*, is undoubtedly among the most important films of the nascent twenty-first century. Both films are in conversation with Lynch's Part 8.

40 A porousness even further highlighted by the deaths of *Twin Peaks* artists in proximity to *The Return*, among them composers Krzysztof Penderecki and Angelo Badalamenti himself; singers Julee Cruise and Jimmy Scott; icon of the entire late twentieth century, David Bowie; actors Miguel Ferrer, Warren Frost, Peggy Lipton, the great Harry Dean Stanton, and the beloved Log Lady played by Catherine Coulson, whose final scenes were memorial scenes, scenes of her own dying, filmed on the precipice of death while in hospice care—a real and poetic goodbye from inside the fiction of *Twin Peaks*.

41 All images are simultaneously real and unreal now, aren't they? Now that all images are possible.

42 *The Blade Runner* replicant test.

43 *Six Drawing Lessons*, a title bearing only homonymous relation to Lynch's first film, the 1967 student project *Six Men Getting Sick*, a wonderfully imaginative and stylized animated drawing which does in fact merit great comparison to the drawings, animations, animated drawings, and theatrical interventions comprising Kentridge's own body of work.

44 William Kentridge, *Six Drawing Lessons* (Harvard University Press, 2014), 27.

45 Kentridge, *Six Drawing Lessons*, 27.

46 Kentridge, *Six Drawing Lessons*, 16.

47 Kentridge, *Six Drawing Lessons*, 32.

48 Or perhaps, finally—it is the image that has harnessed agency now, and not its maker, its keeper, or its seer, but the undead algorithmic organism of projector-cave, the viral image itself as agent. Theft of cold fire, cold fusion.

49 Transcendent thanatos I borrow from writer Sterling Holywhitemountain.

50 On the June 25, 2017 streaming premiere of Part 8.

51 A sonic relief here from the stock Hollywood content of the omnipresent BRAAAM tone, or *Inception* sound, capitalized and relied on by Nolan, Zimmer, et al.

52 Paused out here, with the remote.

53 Lynch and Malick were film school colleagues at the American Film Institute in Los Angeles.

54 Suprematist.

55 Along with the sublime and epic historical melancholy of Bob Dylan's *Murder Most Foul*, also released during Covid.

56 Exemplified by the merchandising of those increasingly accurate, transparent *Twin Peaks*-font window decals indicating that everything outside that window has been "Directed by David Lynch."

57 Alongside the red-curtained waiting room, of course, itself detected in its earliest incarnation in the seminal *Eraserhead*; *Inland Empire*'s living room of anthropomorphic rabbits, *Lost Highway*'s roadhouse exploding in reverse; and countless examples in *The Return*.

58 Walker Evans, *Gibson Motor Company Gas Station with Attendant Leaning on Pump, Reedsville, West Virginia*, June 1935.

59 And its synchronicity with "The Farm," a space adjacent to the mythic room above a convenience store that in Minute 4 Ray tells Mr. C he would like to reach in order to rejoin his gang.

60 Garmonbozia, the cryptically referred to sustenance of the tormented lechers and incubi of the Black Lodge.

61 Super America, the hyperbolic gas station minimart franchise of my 1980s midwestern teenage years, wherein all food products, radioactive and radioactive-proof alike, might be

obtained, for the road. *Super America*: that glowing neon
Black Lodge fossil fuel depot convenience store radiating
psyop into the broad daylight night.

62   Kafka's, Lynch's—

63   And the split atom of its predatory, maleficent dyad: shame
     and sexual violence.

64   As she is so named in the credits to Part 8.

65   *"Sometimes my arms bend back."*

66   As before, the material "pain and sorrow" of garmonbozia
     was related to artist Trevor Paglen's use of the nuclear blast-
     produced mineral Trinitite (also possibly comprising the Twin
     Peaks owl ring); here Lynch's attention to the experiment's
     viscous expectorant is reminiscent of artist Matthew Barney's
     frequent use of substances such as tapioca, beeswax, and
     petroleum jelly, or Vaseline, as a cinematic sculptural
     vernacular.

67   A goop also not entirely unrelated in texture, viscosity, and
     pseudo-supernatural quality to its contemporary counterpart
     as wellness—or *Goop*—the neoliberal napalm of a weaponized
     psychological real estate.

68   *"Hawk, my log is turning to gold,"* the Log Lady
     communicated in her final message to the Twin Peaks Sheriff's
     Department—and to us all—signaling on the threshold to
     death the alchemy from the fire that her log had endured to
     the mythic or spiritual state it was now attaining.

69   Also resembling the purest, honeyest of bee breads, or
     ambrosia, the food of honey bees and the food of the gods, or
     the antithesis of garmonbozia.

70   Coffee, pie, garmonbozia, and music occupying the ordinal
     positions.

71   Filled with *purple rain*. A reservoir of purple rain. The
     symbolic enzymatic watershed of blood-brain barrier
     conducting and protecting the psychic content of the White
     Lodge, electrified by Trinity; as all of the ultraviolet and
     vaporwave 1980s culminating in *Twin Peaks*, and indeed *Twin
     Peaks* itself, as will be made clear, are possessed by Trinity.
     (*Mommy, why does everybody have a bomb?*)

72 Heimat, home or homeland associated with German
    Romanticism and German Nationalism.

73 Susan Sontag, "Fascinating Fascism," *Under the Sign of Saturn*
    (Farrar, Straus and Giroux, 1980), 77. Sontag's essay on Leni
    Riefenstahl is deeply worth reading in full. As we know, the
    impact and influence of Riefenstahl's pioneering ambition,
    sinister ambiguity, and murderous, genocidal patronage are
    world-historical and far-reaching and are directly visible, of
    course, in the fascist assemblies, pageantry, and design of *Star
    Wars*.

74 Brutalist, of course! But reportedly inspired by Lynch's own
    painting *Mr. Jim's Home by the Sea*.

75 A cryptic design vernacular here also in association with the
    euphemistic and anachronistic ambiguity of "The Gadget," as
    the atomic bomb in development was affectionately called by
    its makers.

76 And Steampunk adjacent.

77 Played by the beloved Carel Struycken and credited in Part 8
    as "???????."

78 David Lynch in conversation with Mark Cousins. *Scene by
    Scene*. BBC. 1999.

79 The eye of the duck, Lynch's anecdotal metaphor for the
    compositional button of detail that ties a scene of conflicting
    speeds together, or the single scene that brings an entire film
    into balance. *Scene by Scene* with Mark Cousins. BBC. 1999.

80 A swooning *Slow 30s Room* by Lynch and Dean Hurley.

81 A critical mass of apocalypse detonating concentrically
    into the future and the past; a psychic shockwave rippling
    from Trinity outward, into the 1980s, beyond which there
    are only looping forgeries of time (genres, appropriations,
    recapitulations, remakes, sequels, and units of content as
    parcels of psychic real estate); the massively distributed
    hyperobject of all *Thoughts & Prayers* as the thermonuclear
    singularity of an algorithmic, archival super-density—not the
    end of history, to restate Virilio, but the obliteration (or total
    disorientation) of a temporal geography. A trauma of total
    poetry as the totally replicant real.

82 Not unlike the ornate Strand Theatre of my Ohio childhood hometown.

83 *"Ideas!"* as Lynch might say.

84 The square cinema format was standard in the silent film era and on television until the proliferation of high-definition TVs of the twenty-first century.

85 An interesting detail: that while the film image has been paused, the projection shutter is still spinning, giving the impression that while events have been suspended, time itself carries on. The implication being that the Fireman has not simply paused a playback of events but has instead retroactively suspended the progression of events themselves by adding more of the targeted frame to the original timeline itself, a replication of the paused frame ad infinitum—so that he may intervene. A subtle demonstration of the elasticity and impressionism of the cinematic real is borne out in the furcated temporal superstructure of *The Return*, as a reflection of shattered minds and hearts. The repetition of frames (as units of time) reveals the paradoxical narrative discrepancy that no matter how many interventions, alterations, alternations, duplications, or amputations may be enacted on the timeline by conspiratorial or editorial means, the memory of events impressed upon that temporal nervous system remains, no matter how buried or faint—as the memory of wood. While Laura may have disappeared from the timeline by memorial intervention, her pain is yet there, as a phantom limb in that Ghostwood Forest, remembering.

86 *The Fireman* by Angelo Badalamenti.

87 Historically, mythic and psychological meanings of the golden sphere or golden ball are legion, but most, of course, invoke some narrative inflection of the pure, solar intention and expression of the uncorrupted spirit, the life-giving energy of an unbounded generosity.

88 The year of my own high school graduation.

89 Another steampunk inflection in the idiosyncratic CGI imagining of this retro-temporal contraption out-of-time; but there is no patronizing contrivance toward the craft-speak of believable world-building here, that is, steampunk genre, or

the convention of aesthetic continuity. Rather, it is the free rigor of design elements that comprises a world-specificity that neither defies nor requires a continuity of belief. In this case: a July 16, 1945 interior design adjacency, accessed via a 2016 irruption into a terminally 1989 alternate timeline. Again, a narrative in which the artistry is the plot, simultaneously centripetal and centrifugal—sonically, sculpturally, and temporally concentric from each cinematic coordinate plotted along a hypertextual timeline. *It's happening again.*

90　The orb of Laura herself, in what would ultimately constitute the archetypal transmission of a tragically sacrificial icon, was sent to Earth as a luminescence capable of drawing out, absorbing, defeating, or otherwise suffering the abominable, misogynistic force of Bob. Or—alternately, as has also been suggested, the generated orb of Laura's doppelgänger, Carrie Page, sent to replace Laura Palmer on an alternate timeline (and therefore end her suffering too), thereby extinguishing Bob from the timeline (in which Bob-as-Leland had writhed and survived) via Leland's alternate anguished suicide over Laura's disappearance in an alternate 1989. What can this possibly mean—in words or on-screen? A fractured digression of split and alternate narrative timelines in the effort to preemptively divert the suffering of the to-be-corrupted child. The visage of the golden sphere. *What year is this?* Ever, the sorrow of time within time within time within time, searched, but not to be recovered. But to try—by the artistry of generative witness. *Twin Peaks* as *The Return* is the epic and serial momento mori of twentieth-century Americana, passing through the violent taxidermy of its own hallucinatory euphoria and into the perpetually reanimating nightmare of itself, looping and glitching as violently unreal. *"I am dead yet I live."* Yet still we live, shining, glitching, looping, crying, and trying.

91　Again bearing comparison to the set pieces of Matthew Barney's *Cremaster Cycle* as energy-conducting organs, and, as ever, to their senior cinematic psychonaut, Alejandro Jodorowski.

92　The spectacular 1927 Baroque Revival style theatre. Jarringly—but not entirely at odds with the radical disruptions of the *Twin Peaks* timeline—the theatre is now an Apple Store.

93   The residence of Laura Palmer doppelgänger Carrie Page.

94   As in the floor sweeping scene to *Green Onions* by Booker T.
     & the M.G.'s in Part 7, or the smoking scene in Part 9 of *The
     Return*—both clocking in at over two minutes—that seem
     to infuse Scorsese, Fassbinder, and Manuel Oliveira into a
     luxuriant pedestrian homage to cinema for the sake of cinema
     all its own.

95   Highlighting again the brilliant work of sound supervisors
     Dean Hurley and Ron Eng in collaboration with Lynch as
     sound designer.

96   Autonomous sensory meridian response, now popularized as
     a genre of physiological experience, is a component of social
     media's endlessly vivisecting properties.

97   A mere 15 miles from Los Alamos, New Mexico, according
     to *Twin Peaks: The Final Dossier*, the extended ephemera by
     Mark Frost, Lynch's *Twin Peaks* co-writer.

98   An emergency symptomatic of the super-structural explosion
     (and meltdown) of content, of which *The Return* itself was
     exemplary and by which it was indeed even possible at all.

99   Bob Dylan, "A Hard Rain's a-Gonna Fall," *The Freewheelin'
     Bob Dylan*, Columbia, 1963.

100 Allen Ginsberg, *Howl and Other Poems* (City Lights Books,
     1956).

101 Again, *it's happening again.*

102 Facilitated by the owner-operator of those means at his full
     surrogacy, service, and disposal.

103 https://en.wikipedia.org/wiki/Colorless_green_ideas_sleep_
     furiously re: Noam Chomsky, *Syntactic Structures* (Mouton &
     Co., 1957). According to Wikipedia, Chomsky composed and
     published the sentence *Colorless green ideas sleep furiously*
     variously between 1955 and 1957, around the time of the
     Woodman's hypnotic, weaponized broadcast..

104 ^^ [And this was (Trump's) secret and vastly misunderstood
     power, the magic of language—his shamanic performance.
     His spell: to relieve Americans of shame. A power not to be
     underestimated. At every station on the spectrum of class,
     even at the extremes—to give Americans permission to live in

the America in which they actually live, and not some other country, but this one. I will shoulder your shame for you, for I have none. I will be criminal for you, for we are all criminals. I will conduct and exorcise all obscenity for I am obscenity. For I am television and I am the end of television. Like all slogans, as a category of language, *Make America Great Again* is not a promise or a premonition of a futurity, but a psychological deflection and unburdening into being unashamed of now, of the great euphoric and criminal casino of Super America exactly as it is, in all its feral poetry, obscene hyperbole, criminal grift, and actual history; releasing pressure from their skulls so that it may all come slopping to the ground (scurrying away with a *thingness* all its own); as always—with such tribal reliability—by providing an Other. Even if that Other is oneself.]

105   A narrative confirmation we only have access to via *The Final Dossier*, the extended ephemera of Mark Frost, Lynch's *Twin Peaks* co-writer, highlighting the deeply speculative narrative of *Twin Peaks*: a narrative that, in the discrepancy between the viewer's encounter with it and a proof of it, may or may not be happening at all.

106   After Timothy Morton, *Humankind* (Verso, 2017), and their insight into the degenerate demons and fiends and succubi, the impish denizens of the red-curtained waiting room, the room above a convenience store, the Black and White Lodges.

107   Increasingly and reliably demonstrable in the Jerry Springer-style small screen roundtables of expert, journalist, and analyst performers and stagings presented by CNN, Fox News, et al., as a reality show inside a reality inside the reality show of the now incessant and perpetually unreal political campaign season. A cycle of *worlding* that is subsequently and consequently reality? Reality show? Fiction? Nonfiction? Even happening at all?

108   Sarah Palmer is an ouroboros, ingesting the symbolic origin story of her future self. As all that has come before, it is art finally that answers to the uncanny reflection of art, swallowing itself over and over and over again. In my own cinematic novel *The Glacier* (Two Dollar Radio, 2015), a tiny holographic atomic blast glitching as a looping mushroom

cloud is followed by a mutant creature entering the mouth of someone sleeping, an irradiated iridescent cockroach—the Kafkan scarab—is swallowed by the poet as proof of his words. An uncanny similitude with details of Part 8 of *The Return*, pointing toward Lynch's mantra that the ideas are all in there, out there waiting to be fished from a kind of Platonic pool, as the very water of that pool itself, perhaps a future primordial soup yet assembling this very moment of our times, which we have already had access to beyond the black star that has generated us. If something happens once, it has never happened at all. If it happens twice, as the nothingness of its sequel, it happens eternally. For the time in which we live lies at the intersection of all other times, but we live in the time that we live and that is all.

Postscript

1 Just a few hours after turning in this manuscript, the world learned of David Lynch's death. The outpouring came in a great wave, itself a kind of temporal monument to the shockwave of his being and his passing. The next morning there was wind, and the air was clean and clear and filled with light, and the brightest blue skies all the way—*for you, absolute giant. Of a country, of the cosmos. Radiant. May you dream upon a river of stars.*

INDEX

aesthetic terror 9
American cultural economy
    2, 5
Anderson, Michael J. 44
Anton Chigurh (*No Country
    for Old Men*) 26
apocalypse
    as media mode 49, 58–9
    Trinity Test, as origin
        of American
        apocalypse 9–11
Apocalypse Now! 4, 9
apocalyptic kitsch 3
artificial intelligence (AI) 1,
    24, 25, 27, 56, 58
Arri Amira camera, digital
    realism use 29
avant-garde cinema 10

Badalamenti, Angelo 14, 111,
    116
Bad Cooper 21–7, 31, 51
Bardem, Javier 26
Barney, Matthew 117
Basket Building
    (Longaberger) 2
Baudrillard, Jean 49
Black Lodge 15, 35, 46,
    72

black magic, of language 1,
    94
Blade Runner (Roy Batty) 25,
    58
Blood Meridian 24, 60
Bowie, David 38, 111
Brechtian alienation effect 26
Burrough, William S. 5

Cassavetes, John 19–32
Chernobyl (Elephant's Foot
        metaphor) 10, 57
Chomsky, Noam 98
Chrysler LeBaron, surreal
        celebrity encounter 44–5
cinematic illumination 12
code/coordinates 20–4
cognitive dissonance 3, 61,
    102
communication 98
Coppola, Francis Ford 4
cosmic fear 7–9, 11, 21, 24,
    36, 42, 56, 61, 74, 82
cosmic psychosis 42
cosmic symbolism 67
Coulson, Catherine 112
Cousins, Mark 114
Crewdson, Gregory 17
Cruise, Julee 111

cultural idealism   5

The Day After (TV movie,
     1983)   5–6
Deming, Peter   29
Dick, Philip K.   5
digital cinematography   19–20
doppelgänger
     Bad Cooper's emergence as
          false self   21–2
     as cosmic and narrative
          threat   24
     identity split and inner
          corruption   22
     time distortion and Cooper's
          timeline confusion   23
dramatic realism   5
drone advertising   78
Dunham, Duwayne   30

electricity (Lynchian)
     disrupts logic of space and
          time   17
     symbolic conductor of souls
          and narrative   14
Eng, Ron   117
Eraserhead   3, 74, 76
evil/demonic agency
     Bob as disembodied
          physiological form   35
     systemic and parahuman evil
          in American culture   40–
          1

fear
     aesthetic fear   9
     cosmic fear, *see* cosmic fear
     narrative fear   8
     ontological fear   9
Ferrer, Miguel   111

fire/smoke
     cinematic combustion and
          visual energy   22
     Trinity Test as symbolic
          ignition   53–5, 70–1
font as narrative (*Twin
     Peaks/Star Wars*)
     14–15
fourth wall/ fifth wall
     (theatrical *vs.*
     psychological)   16–17
Friedrich, Caspar David   54
frogmoth (hatchling
     creature)   101
     amphibian/insect
          fusion from atomic
          mutation   88
     hybrid CGI being and
          ontological terror   88
Frost, Mark   16
Frost, Warren   112

geography collapse   78
Ginsberg, Allen   97
Glazer, Jonathan   111
Great Serpent Mound of
     Ohio   2
Guan, Frank   108

Hauer, Rutger   108
HELL IS REAL (billboard as
     cinematic land art)   1–2,
     11
Hering, David   109
Herzog, Werner   62
Hido, Todd   17
Hopper, Dennis   108
Hurley, Dean   117
hybrid fears   9
hyper-subjectivity   61

iconographic cairns   11, 19
illusion and illumination   65
imposter syndrome   26
intimacy   7, 9, 56, 57
    cataclysmic intimacy   56
    and isolation   58
    Lynchian intimacy   9
    paradoxical intimacy   9
    stereoscopic vision   21

Jeff Koons   2

Kafka, Franz   111
Kansas   4
"The Kekulé Problem"
    (McCarthy, Cormac)   23
Kentridge, William   63
Kubrick, Stanley   57

Lang, Fritz   77
language
    artificial sentience of   24
    as cinematic
        unconscious   24
    conspiracy of narrative
        99
    theatrical language   34
Laura Palmer, portrait of   14,
    23, 42, 85, 86
Lipton, Peggy   112
Lynch, David   3, 5, 9, 17–20,
    45, 58, 87, 114, 119
Lynchian visual symbol
    electricity   14
    red curtains   16–17

MacLachlan, Kyle   26
Manzano, Frank   25
McCarthy, Cormac   59, 60,
    107, 108

Kekulé Problem and
    language origins   23–4
    Trinity as ontological
        bomb   60
Morton, Timothy   118
Murphy, Cillian   61
Muybridge   21

narrative terror   8
Nine Inch Nails (performance)
    performance breaks fourth
        wall   48
    Trent Reznor as apocalyptic
        ferryman   49
No Exit   18
Nolan, Christopher   61

ontological terror   9
Oppenheimer, Joshua   111
Oppenheimer, J. Robert   59

Paglen, Trevor   52
Palmer, Sarah   118
panic, as mystical state   8
paranormal electricities   79
Park, Briscoe   17
Penderecki, Krzysztof   53, 111
perception   17
post-apocalyptic landscape   2,
    10
post-human language   24–5
psychopathic archetype   27

Queiroz, Jorge   69

Ray, Nicholas   89
real estate, of cinematic
    object   42, 62, 78, 102
reality *vs.* fiction   5–7, 13, 14,
    24, 110

The Return   25
Reznor, Trent   47–49, 51, 67
The Road   107
Rombes, Nick   106

Samuels, David   49, 110
Scott, Jimmy   46, 111
Sherman, Cindy   17
Sirk, Douglas   89
social media   10
social psychosis   42
Sontag, Susan   77
sound
    cinematic combustion
      (fire, noise, death,
      apocalypse)   70–1
    electric buzz as narrative
      loop and psychic
      key   13–14
    Penderecki's *Threnody*
      as sonic trauma of
      Trinity   53
sound of electricity   13
Sphere   49
Stanton, Harry Dean   112
Starr, J. R.   38, 46, 47
Star Wars   3, 14, 15, 56, 57

The Strand Theatre   3
streaming culture/seriality   10
Struycken, Carel   114
Sycamore Trees   46
symbolic terror   6–7

The Thing   9
Thompson, Hunter S.   44
Threnody for the Victims
    of Hiroshima
    (Penderecki)   53, 55, 70
trauma   5–6
Trinity Test   9, 10, 55, 60, 61,
    89, 110, 111
Trump, D.   99
Twin Peaks   4, 109
Twin Peaks: The Return
    (Lynch)   5, 7, 9, 13, 100

unconscious, cinematic   23,
    24, 32, 42, 96, 102, 103

Villeneuve, Denis   58
Virilio, Paul   7, 11, 56
Voight-Kampff Test   63

The Wizard of Oz   4, 5

www.ingramcontent.com/pod-product-compliance
Lightning Source LLC
Chambersburg PA
CBHW060319120126

38084CB00007B/29